pure
pilates

pure
pilates

Pure Pilates
Michael King
First published in 2000 by Mitchell Beazley
an imprint of Octopus Publishing Group Ltd
2–4 Heron Quays, London E14 4JP

ISBN 1840002662

A CIP catalogue record for this book is available from
the British Library

Executive Editor	Rachael Stock
Executive Art Editor	Emma Boys
Project Editors	Mary Loebig Giles, Frances Williams
Design	Kenny Grant
Production	Nancy Roberts
Picture Research	Helen Stallion, Khali Dhillon
Photography	Ruth Jenkinson
Models	Beth Caterer Simon Spalding

Typeset in Walbaum, Syntax and Versailles
Printed in China by Toppan Printing Company Ltd

For more information on Pilates classes visit Michael King's
website at www.michaelking.co.uk

contents

INTRODUCTION

8   What is Pilates?
10 Why Pilates?
14 Why pure Pilates?
16 Man and mentor
20 Setting your goals
22 Step-by-step plan
26 Preventing pain

VITAL ELEMENTS

32 Concentration
34 Breathing
36 Centering
38 Control
40 Precision
42 Movement
44 Isolation
46 Routine

THE MOVEMENTS

WARM-UPS
50 Swinging
51 Round back,
    Chest stretch
52 One arm circles
53 Double arm circles,
    Toy soldier

THE ESSENTIALS
54 Push-up
56 Swimming
58 Leg pull prone
60 Roll-up
62 Rolling back
63 One leg circle
64 The hundred
66 The seal
67 One leg stretch

68 The saw
69 Shoulder bridge preparation
70 Side kick
71 Spine stretch
72 Spine twist
73 Neutral spine

NEW CHALLENGES
74 The crab
75 Double leg stretch
76 Rocker with open legs
77 Shoulder bridge
78 Side bend
80 Side-kick kneeling
81 The teaser
82 The jack knife
83 Hip twist
84 Scissors
85 The rocker

HIGH INTENSITY
86 The boomerang
87 Neck pull
88 Control balance
89 Leg pull supine
90 The corkscrew
91 Rollover

92 Tips to remember
94 Glossary
95 Index
96 Acknowledgements

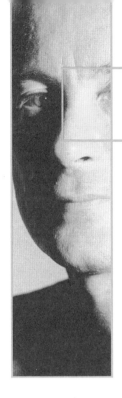

introduction

Pilates is not just a series of exercises, it is a conceptual approach to movement. It will change not only the way you look, but how you feel and think. The technique can be taught in different ways – for strength or relaxation. In Pure Pilates we aim for a balance of both.

Twenty-two years ago I came across Pilates as a dancer at the London School of Contemporary Dance. Though it was part of our daily training, I didn't really understand the importance of it. It wasn't until I began practising Pilates to repair a back injury that I really began to appreciate its power and effectiveness. I loved what it did to heal my body. I was so inspired by the method, I went on to train with Alan Herdman, the first teacher to bring Pilates from America to Britain.

In 1982 I opened my own studio, Body Control, in connection with the newly formed Pineapple Dance Studios in Covent Garden. Two years later I was offered a job in Texas to run the Pilates studio at the Houston Ballet Company, which was set up both for dancers and outside patrons. (During this time I also trained to teach the new Fonda-established aerobics.) I have taught Pilates ever since.

It is so exciting to see the recent boom in popularity that Pilates has enjoyed. From both the experience of my own back injury and my extensive work within the fitness world, I have come to appreciate the true value and significance of the technique. I used to think that becoming hunched up was an inevitable part of the aging process. I now see that how we treat our bodies from day to day can affect how we feel and look as we get older.

My goal is to pass on the information and knowledge that I have picked up over the years and to share the secrets I've found that make this work successful. Pilates is a very varied technique and can be taught in many formats and styles. I believe that through practising pure Pilates we can all achieve better balance, gain leaner bodies and feel more poised and less stressed. Always remember that it just as crucial to master the

vital elements behind the technique as it is to simply perform the movements. Pilates is not just a series of physical exercises but a concept-based routine that will challenge old assumptions. Pilates has been called a 'thinking way of moving'. It involves making a commitment to yourself, your body and your well-being. You can know all the movements and still not properly appreciate Pilates.

The total concept also involves getting enough sleep, eating right and continuing your usual fitness programme. Through the years I've combined my early Pilates training with regular fitness training. Pilates is not an 'instead of' but an 'as well as'. In other words, it doesn't replace your current fitness programmes but is a valuable and necessary addition.

I know that you will find Pilates to be as empowering for you as it has been for me.

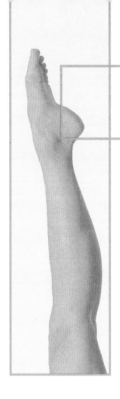

what is pilates?

Pilates offers a different way of thinking about your body. Through practising the movements, you will become more self-aware and better able to take control of your body and your life. Although the technique may at times take you outside your comfort zone, the benefits of this are that you begin to understand and appreciate not only your strengths, but also your weaknesses.

At this, the beginning of a new millennium, there has been a renewed interest in exercise techniques that also acknowledge the power of the mind. Pilates, like Feldenkrais, the Alexander technique and yoga, fall under this mind–body umbrella. All these techniques offer alternative philosophies to conventional thinking about health and fitness.

Mind and movement

Pilates is named after its inventor, Joseph Pilates, who formulated the exercises in the 1920s. There are 34 original Pilates movements. As well as matwork, there are also equipment-based routines. These pieces of equipment, devised by Joseph Pilates himself, have strange and wonderful names such as The Wunda Chair, The Cadillac and the Pedi-Pul. In a traditional Pilates studio you work half the session on the equipment and the other half performing matwork exercises. Each offers different benefits. If you can get to a Pilates studio, you will find this out for yourself: working on equipment is great. Alternatively, if this is impossible, the matwork exercises provide an extremely thorough programme in the convenience of your own home.

Beauty and benefit

Pilates has been around for the last seventy years but has recently drawn much media coverage. Many Hollywood stars have given the technique their endorsement. Madonna, for example, affirmed that Pilates is the only way to exercise. As a result of such public praise, Pilates is no longer an exclusive secret of the rich and famous. What once might have seemed like a strange cult activity is now a popular class in health clubs the world over. While some people become interested in Pilates for its cosmetic body-

Celebrity endorsement

Pilates has always attracted a star following. Initially Lauren Bacall and Gregory Peck were interested in the technique. Now a whole new generation has embraced Pilates, including actress Jodie Foster, dancer Wayne Sleep, tennis player Pat Cash and pop icon Madonna.

sculpting effects, others come to it through referrals by their physiotherapist or medical practitioner. In particular, Pilates has been the first exercise choice for many, like myself, who have injured their backs. I see Pilates as an excellent preventative technique that will strengthen your body against potential injury. It cannot, however, act as a replacement for medical advice. If you have a physical problem, find out what is going on before attempting the Pilates movements. Specific problems should be addressed by a qualified therapist.

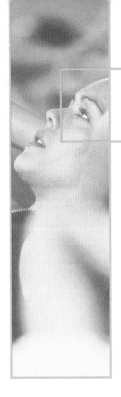

why pilates?

Pilates is unique in that it will systematically exercise all the muscle groups in your body, the weak as well as the strong. It combines the focus on suppleness that you find in yoga with the emphasis on strength building found in the gym. In this way, it aims to create balance and natural poise, taking into consideration all the factors involved in the maintenance of a healthy body.

People often wonder how Pilates exercises can change body shape. The secret is simple. Pilates movements gently stretch the muscles, pulling them into leaner and longer shapes. It might help if I explain what I mean by the term 'longer'. Bodybuilders increase their muscle bulk by overloading muscles, tearing fibres and causing them to rebuild. In the process the muscle becomes shorter and thicker. Pilates is different because it does exactly the opposite. It works by continually stretching your limbs and torso, ensuring muscles become longer and leaner rather than shorter and thicker.

New thinking

It is now recognised that the regular fitness regimes we have been doing for so many years are not so much wrong as incomplete. We have made exercise very safe: people no longer injure

themselves in the gym, but do pull muscles at home or work when they lift something heavy out of a car or pick up their small child. This is because standard exercise does not prepare the body for these activities. Traditionally, exercise and strength training has compartmentalised the body, training individual body parts, such as the bicep in a bicep curl or the quadricep in a leg extension. But we have not trained our body parts to work together, in synergy.

United we stand

Think of an orchestra rehearsing; the brass section might practise in one room and the strings rehearse in another. The symphony only comes together when all parts of the orchestra play together. Standard exercise keeps sections of the orchestra practising separately. While each section may be strong and technically

Lines of symmetry

The body is built along lines of symmetry and every exertion is subject to checks and balances. Lift your left arm up until it is horizontal and hold it there. Put your other hand to the right-hand side of your back. You should be able to feel the muscles in your back clenching.

skilled, they still need to rehearse together in order to make music and achieve complete balance.

Functional fitness

'Functional fitness' is a hot topic today. Magazines are full of articles on the subject. But what does it mean? Let me explain by going back to the gym to look at the regular seated bench press. A seated bench press involves sitting on the equipment and pushing the weight in front of you. On a good day you might be able to push 40, 50, possibly 60 pounds. However, if you were to

move one inch forward of the back support, you would only be able to push around a third of the weight. Here, without the support of the chair behind you, you can measure the true extent of your functional strength.

Sitting up and listening

I have come to realise the extent to which the shape of our bodies reflects our day-to-day activities. Whether we are aware of it or not, we literally shape ourselves. Those with the best posture in the world are the traditional Japanese. Why? They have no backs to their chairs. Here in the Western world we have made life very comfortable by designing the most supportive chair, car and airline seat. We do not ask much of the body in daily activities. In the morning we go from sitting behind our breakfast table, to sitting behind our steering wheel, to sitting behind our desk, to sitting behind our lunch table. Then it is back to the desk, home in the car again, sitting in front of the TV, back to bed. Three times a week we might go to the gym and do sit-ups hoping this will bring balance to our lives. Is it any surprise that 80% of us will experience back pain in our lives?

Train for life

Modern living has made life so easy that we don't ask our backs to work. Sadly, in contemporary Japan, the young Japanese now have the same postural problems that we suffer. We talk about going to the gym to train, but we are constantly training our bodies

to behave in other ways during the remaining hours of the day when we are not at the gym.

With modern life leaving so little room for an integrated programme of exercise, it is no wonder that there has been a significant movement in recent years towards mind and body techniques. Only these disciplines offer the opportunity of using our bodies in a complete way. We exercise to improve our 'quality of life'. Yet what does this mean? It means we want our daily lives to be improved and enriched. We want to be able, for example, to carry the shopping, lift a child, move a wardrobe or push a car if it breaks down. It is these kinds of daily activity that demand functional strength.

Professional posture

Functional exercises are exercises designed to be appropriate to the needs of everyday living. Many of the people who come to my class at lunchtime sit behind a desk all day long. As a Pilates instructor I train them to sit (strengthening their core stability) since they are 'professional sitters'. There is little purpose in focusing on the biggest bicep or the strongest leg. It is not that these things are not important and should not be worked on, but my priority has to be on strengthening their body for the longest activity of the day. Pilates will develop the areas that need attention and build strength in our weakest areas. Building strength in the abdomen is vital to most daily activities as it is this area which provides core stability.

Symmetry and synergy

I like to compare using the body to putting up a tent. Our movements are comprised of a series of checks and balances; exertion on the right side of the body will be compensated for on the left. For a tent to be secure there has to be an equal amount of tension on both front and back ropes. If the tension is too tight, the ropes are in danger of snapping and there is no flexibility against winds. If we always pull on one side, our 'tent' of muscles will veer out of balance. If we only train our abdominals and not our back, then we are pulling on just one section of our 'tent strings'. Only when there is equal tension between front and back, our right sides and our left, can true stability and balance be achieved.

An integrated approach

Our bodies demand an integrated approach whereby no single muscle is developed at the expense of another. The body is built on lines of symmetry and the Pilates exercise technique acknowledges and exploits this fact. The daily habits of our lives often mitigate against an integrated approach and we find ourselves leading sedentary working lives in offices where there is little scope for using our full physical potential. Medical conditions such as 'repetitive strain' can result. Pilates can redress the balance and help us to become more aware of what we unconsciously do to our bodies. Through self-awareness we can identify and alter our bad habits.

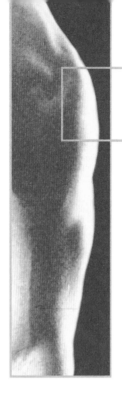

why pure pilates?

The original, authentic matwork exercises, as devised by Joseph Pilates, are more taxing than the simplified moves advocated by many teachers. You will have to work up to pure Pilates movements gradually, using the easier alternatives we offer. But if you want real results, original is best.

Pilates offers a whole-body workout that challenges your body like no other exercise. When Joseph Pilates devised the original matwork exercises, he did not intend to spare us any effort. Even the fittest of athletes will find some of the original moves very difficult to complete, simply because they require the control and coordination of muscles that few of us are accustomed to using.

Easing your way in

In order to make life easier for beginners, many teachers have devised diluted versions of the movements. There is a real place for this. Not everybody can go straight to the crab or the leg pull without gradually easing the muscles into use. This is why I have listed alternative moves alongside all the main moves in the book – to allow you to begin on an easier version. There may be some people for whom

physical constraints or medical conditions mean that they cannot progress onto pure Pilates. This is fine. Part of Pilates is knowing your limits and working within them. However, if you are fairly fit and flexible, you will find that you can move on to the advanced exercises more quickly. Joseph Pilates developed the movements to challenge muscles, knowing that for you, as for him, it would lead to perfect toning. These exercises are designed to elongate and stretch the muscles in order to create a sleek and leaner look.

Pure is best

The pure forms of the movements give you the best results as they are more intense. For this reason I have presented the pure form first and the alternatives afterwards. I believe it is always good to see what you are aiming for. Although there is no one single right or wrong way to teach or practise

Who's right or wrong?

By knowing pure Pilates you'll have a reference point to understand the variations on the movements taught by different instructors. Variations offer a range of distinct effects and benefits. The specialist knowledge and background of the instructors determines how they interpret the Pilates movements. It is a testament to the effectiveness of the original technique that so many others have learnt from it and gone on to devise their own programmes.

Pilates, it is these pure movements that have best stood the test of time. If we are physically capable, we should aspire to achieve the original moves. Attaining good results will also involve understanding the principles, the vital elements that make the discipline what it is. In this book we have presented these elements one by one so that you can understand the full meaning and benefits of Pilates matwork.

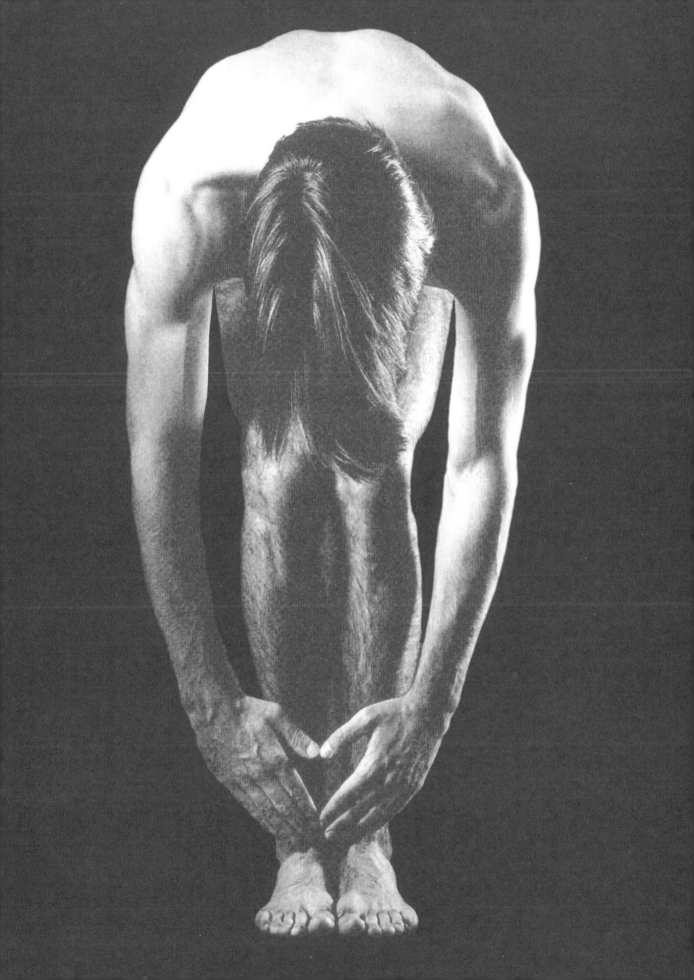

man and mentor

Prone to childhood illness, Joseph Pilates refused to let poor physical health cloud his future. Determined to fulfil his potential, he studied bodybuilding, gymnastics, boxing and diving until he had mastered them all. After years of study, he developed an approach to fitness that would change the way people viewed physical exercise. This is his intriguing story.

Joseph Humbertus Pilates was born near Dussledorf, Germany, in 1880. He suffered from a range of debilitating conditions throughout his childhood including rickets, asthma and rheumatic fever. Determined to overcome his poor physical health, he devoted himself to the task of becoming as fit and strong as was humanly possible. This determination was characteristic of Pilates' spirited and forceful personality. His early fierce reaction to illness would inform all his future enterprises.

Excelling in fitness

In his youth Pilates studied and became proficient at numerous sports and fitness activities, including skiing, gymnastics, diving and bodybuilding. By the time he was 14 years old, he was in such good shape that he was able to work as a model for anatomical charts. In 1912, Pilates moved from Germany to England

where he earned a living in a wide variety of jobs that required him to be in peak physical condition. He worked as a boxer, circus performer and a self-defence trainer of English detectives.

Exercise innovator

When World War I broke out Pilates was interned because of his nationality. He was held in camps in Lancaster and the Isle of Man. While there he acted as a physician to the other men. It seemed a natural step for him eventually to take responsibility for the health of the other interns and he began training them in physical fitness. It was then that he first improvised making fitness equipment, removing the springs from the beds and attaching them to the walls above the beds so that patients could exercise while lying down. After the war, Pilates continued his fitness programmes back in Germany, in Hamburg,

where he worked with the police force before being drafted into the army. By 1926, disenchanted with Germany, he decided to move to America. On the ship to New York he met a nurse called Clara, the woman he was to later marry.

Guru to dancers

Soon after arriving in New York, Pilates set up his first exercise studio at 939 Eighth Avenue. Though little is known about the early years of his business, by the 1940s Joe had achieved a certain amount of notoriety amongst the city's dance community. 'At some time or other,' reported *Dance Magazine* in its February 1956 issue, 'virtually every dancer in New York had meekly submitted to the spirited instruction of Joe Pilates.' By the early 1960s, Pilates could count many of New York's finest dancers among his clients. George Balanchine, one of ballet's foremost choreographers and

co-founder of the New York City Ballet, worked out 'at Joe's,' as he called it, and also invited Pilates to instruct the young dancers of his acclaimed ballet company. 'Pilates', as it was now becoming known, was catching on and becoming very popular outside New York City as well. As the *New York Herald Tribune* noted in 1964, 'in dance classes around the United States, hundreds of young students limber up daily with an exercise they know as a Pilates, without knowing that the word has a capital P, and a living, right-breathing namesake.'

The next generation
Just two of Joe's students, Carola Trier and Bob Seed, are known to have opened their own Pilates studios while Joe was still living.

Trier had an extensive dance background. She had found her way to the United States after escaping being sent to a Nazi concentration camp in France by becoming a contortionist in a circus show. She discovered Pilates in 1940, when a non-stage injury effectively curtailed her performing career as a dancer. Joe Pilates assisted Trier in opening her own studio in the late 1950s. Bob Seed was another story. A former hockey player turned Pilates enthusiast, Seed opened his own studio across town from Joe's. He tried poaching some of Joe's clients by opening his studio early in the morning. It was rumoured that, as a result of this betrayal, Joe visited Seed with a gun and warned him to get out of town. Seed promptly left.

The legacy
When Joe passed away in 1967, he was 87 years old. He left no will and had designated no successor to carry on the Pilates exercise work. Nevertheless, due to the popularity and effectiveness of the technique, his work was destined to continue.

Clara, Joe's wife, continued to operate what was already known as the Pilates Studio in New York and Romana Kryzanowska, a former student who had been instructed by Pilates in the 1940s, became its director in the 1970s.

Other students of Pilates went on to open their own studios. Ron Fletcher, a dancer who trained under Martha Graham, the central figure of the modern dance movement, studied and consulted with Joe from the 1940s in connection with a chronic knee ailment. Fletcher eventually opened his own Pilates studio in Los Angeles in 1970, where he attracted many of Hollywood's brightest stars. Clara was particularly enamoured with Ron and gave her blessing for him to carry on the Pilates work and name.

Like Carola Trier, Fletcher brought numerous innovations and advancements to the Pilates technique. His evolving variations on Pilates were inspired both by his years in modern dance and by another mentor, ballet instructor Yeichi Nimura.

Kathy Grant and Lolita San Miguel were also students of Joe who went on to become teachers. Grant took over the direction at the Bendel's studio in 1972, while San Miguel went on to teach Pilates at Ballet Concierto de Puerto Rica in San Juan, Puerto Rico. In 1967, just before Joe's death, both Grant and San Miguel were awarded degrees by the State University of New York to teach Pilates. These two are believed to be the only Pilates practitioners ever to be certified officially by Joe himself.

His wider influence

In order to formulate his ideas, Joseph Pilates studied across a range of different sports and exercise disciplines from both the East and the West. He was most influenced by the ideas of the ancient Greeks and often quoted the admonition that in life we should abide by the rule 'Not too little, not too much'. He was one of the first people to promote an holistic approach. He looked to the natural world for clues about the human body and spent time, for example, looking closely at the movement of animals.

Joesph Pilates' ideas remain remarkably relevant. He blamed the 'constant pushing, shoving, rushing, crowding and wild scrambling all so characteristic of our day' for many of our mental and bodily ills. 'This too fast pace,' he asserted, 'is plainly reflected in our manner of standing, walking, sitting, eating and even talking and results in our nerves being on edge from morning to night.' This applies more than ever to the busy, stressful lives we lead today.

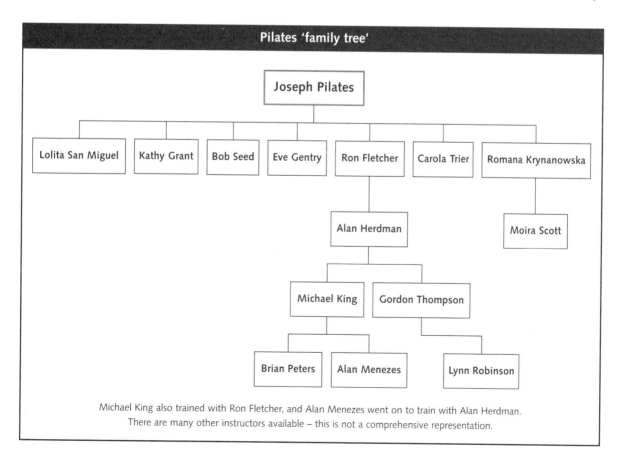

Pilates 'family tree'

Michael King also trained with Ron Fletcher, and Alan Menezes went on to train with Alan Herdman. There are many other instructors available – this is not a comprehensive representation.

setting your goals

Whether your goal is to redefine your body shape, relieve stiffness or build strength, the first step is positive thinking. Pilates will change the shape of your body. I have seen it happen hundreds of times. I have also seen it help relieve back and hip pain and correct postural problems. Believe, practise, and watch it happen!

When I ask my new students what they want to get out of Pilates, the most common answer from the women is 'I want to have a body like Madonna' while the men insist that they 'want a six-pack stomach'. Other goals most often mentioned include the relief of back pain or building strength.

Patience and practise

When I tell people that Pilates will change the shape of their bodies, the most commonly asked question is 'How long will it take for me to see results?'. 'You'll see them instantly' is my reply. If you stand taller on your feet, pull your abdominals in tight and drop your shoulders, immediately you will look so much better! The question really should be 'How long will it take for me to maintain this look without having to think about it?' The answer, realistically, is three to six months of regular practise.

Weighty matters

There is one frequently cited goal that is not achievable by Pilates alone: it will not help you lose weight. If you need to shed pounds, you should do some cardiovascular training 4–5 times per week (I find spin-cycle classes change the shape of body fat distribution most effectively) and follow a suitable nutritional programme. There are many theories on nutrition, but I have found a food combining diet (separating consumption of carbohydrates and protein) and a reduction in fat intake works well for my clients.

Work on weaknesses

It is important to recognise where your strengths and weaknesses lie. By weakness I don't just mean lack of muscular strength. A tight, inflexible back is as problematic as a weak one. Because Pilates exercises balance the body, different movements challenge us in different ways. I find that the movements my students least enjoy are usually the ones they cannot do very well. This often indicates a weakness. Instead of avoiding the exercises you enjoy the least, it is vital to persist.

A new shape

You might never look quite like Madonna, or have the perfect six-pack as a result of practising Pilates, but good posture and longer, leaner muscles will make you look a new person. However, it will take time. We live in a society where we want everything 'now'. Instead, start thinking about your goals in the full knowledge that it is going to take a while for you to reap (and feel) the full benefits. I know it will happen, and I know that you will be delighted with the results.

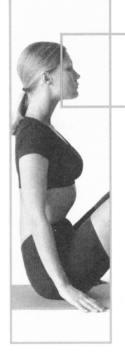

step-by-step plan

The charts on the following pages are designed to help you to put together your own exercise plan. Use them to combine different Pilates movements as you progress through levels of increasing difficulty and intensity. By following these guidelines you will gradually build up your strength and mobility in equal measure. Each exercise challenges muscle groups in a different way.

The charts on the following pages set out the combinations you need to follow in order to create your own Pilates routine. Always start with low intensity variations and only progress on to the harder variations once you feel happy and in control of your movement.

Patience pays

Pilates most benefits those who show the greatest patience. Do not be tempted to cheat and skip ahead to more advanced levels before you are ready. Even the fittest person should start at level one. Only in this way can you learn the base work so necessary to progress to harder exercises. You will know when you are ready to move on when you have fully mastered your breathing.

Do not rush

We live in a world which usually tells us that it is always better to exercise harder and faster to achieve results. But with Pilates the opposite is true. Working slowly and correctly ensures the full use of all our muscles. The same principle is just as applicable in the gym. Slowly lifting up a light weight and carefully letting it down a number of times is far more productive than quickly jacking up a heavy weight and abruptly releasing it. Working slowly ensures you maximize your muscle effectiveness. Make sure you measure your own progress through the various levels by how thoroughly you are able to complete each movement.

Time for yourself

Before you begin, make sure you set a regular time and place for your workout. Some people prefer to exercise in the morning while others feel they are more flexible in the evenings. Always leave enough time to complete the programme properly.

Cross-training

Just because you have started to exercise using the Pilates method, it does not mean that you have to give up on other sports and fitness programmes. On the contrary, your Pilates programme is best served when it is complimented by a form of cardiovascular exercise. Complete low-stress Pilates exercises alongside aerobic ones. You will find Pilates ideal for cross-training because it will correct any postural problem associated with other forms of repetitive exercise. Pilates embraces all the areas that make up a fully integrated approach to fitness; strength, flexibility, motor skills, coordination and relaxation.

Setting your pace

It might take a month or so to perfect each level although every individual's needs are different. Do things at the pace that feels right for you. You should not at any point experience any sudden or severe pain. If you start shaking or sweating, then you are pushing

Essential Exercise Chart

Page	Movement	Emphasis	Level 1	Level 2	Level 3	Level 4
54	THE PUSH-UP	Strength		o	o	o
56	SWIMMING	Strength	o	o	o	o
58	LEG PULL PRONE	Strength				o
60	ROLL-UP	Strength		o	o	o
62	ROLLING BACK	Mobility	o	o	o	o
63	ONE LEG CIRCLE	Mobility	o	o	o	o
64	THE HUNDRED	Strength	o	o	o	o
66	THE SEAL	Mobility			o	o
67	ONE LEG STRETCH	Strength			o	o
68	THE SAW	Mobility			o	o
69	SHOULDER BRIDGE PREP	Mobility	o	o	o	o
70	SIDE KICK	Strength			o	o
71	SPINE STRETCH	Mobility	o	o	o	o
72	SPINE TWIST	Mobility		o	o	o

things too far, too soon. As I have said before, expect your weaknesses to be revealed.

Starting off

Initially, each programme should last around an hour. This amount of time allows for the completion of the first six movements. You should always split your moves into two halves, three for mobility and three for strength. In my classes, most people take around a month or so to master the exercises set out in level one. Aim to complete your exercise plan three or four times a week. After a few weeks, move onto the next level, adding two more strength and mobility moves each time. Introduce new movements slowly if you don't feel you can double up

your exercise plan so quickly. Just how fast you progress through the programme depends on a number of factors including how often you practise each week, for how long, and your physical condition at the start of the programme. Do not despair if sometimes you feel less capable of achieving movements at the higher levels than at other times. It is normal for the body to feel more tired on some days than others. A small amount of regular exercise, correctly performed, is always better than erratic over-exertion. Joseph Pilates asserted that you should attempt at least ten minutes of Pilates a day "without fail". If you can only spare ten minutes, it is best to concentrate on The Hundred and Rolling Back.

Progressing further

As you progress to more intense movements, you will drop some of the basic exercises you mastered at the beginning. This is because some of the beginners movements are built into the more advanced ones. So as you start doing The Seal, you will stop Rolling Back. Similarly, as you begin The Saw you will stop doing The Spine Twist. As before, keep on trying to do six or more exercises during the hour, picking an equal balance of strength and mobility movements from the chart as you progress. Always try to vary your selection and persist with the movements you find difficult. The better you become at doing Pilates exercises, the larger the choice of movement open to you becomes.

New Challenges Exercise Chart

Page	Movement	Emphasis	Level 5	Level 6	Level 7	Level 8
54	THE PUSH-UP	Strength	o	o	o	o
56	SWIMMING	Strength	o	o	o	o
58	LEG PULL PRONE	Strength	o	o	o	o
60	ROLL-UP	Strength	o	o	o	o
62	ROLLING BACK	Mobility				
63	ONE LEG CIRCLE	Mobility	o	o	o	o
64	THE HUNDRED	Strength	o	o	o	o
66	THE SEAL	Mobility	o			
67	ONE LEG STRETCH	Strength	o	o		
68	THE SAW	Mobility	o	o	o	o
69	SHOULDER BRIDGE PREP	Mobility	o	o		
70	SIDE KICK	Strength	o	o	o	
71	SPINE STRETCH	Mobility	o	o	o	o
72	SPINE TWIST	Mobility	o	o	o	o
74	THE CRAB	Mobility	o	o	o	o
75	DOUBLE LEG STRETCH	Strength			o	o
76	ROCKER WITH OPEN LEGS	Mobility		o	o	o
77	SHOULDER BRIDGE	Strength			o	o
78	SIDE BEND	Strength	o	o	o	o
80	SIDE-KICK KNEELING	Strength				o
81	THE TEASER	Strength			o	o
82	JACK KNIFE	Strength				o
83	HIP TWIST	Strength			o	o
84	SCISSORS	Strength	o	o	o	o
85	THE ROCKER	Strength				o

If you have a known medical condition, are pregnant, or have any chronic joint problems, you should consult your doctor before starting any exercise programme. It is not advisable to start Pilates after becoming pregnant unless you have already been training with the technique. A check-up is also advisable if you are aged over 40, if you are overweight or if have not been undertaking any physical exercise for some time. If you experience any chest pains or pain in your back or neck while doing any of the movements, then stop immediately. Drink plenty of fluids after you work out, especially in hot weather. Always wear comfortable clothes that will not restrict your movement.

Advanced Exercise Chart

Page	Movement	Emphasis	Level 9	Level 10	Level 11	Level 12
54	THE PUSH-UP	Strength	o	o	o	o
56	SWIMMING	Strength	o	o	o	o
58	LEG PULL PRONE	Strength	o	o	o	o
60	ROLL-UP	Strength				
62	ROLLING BACK	Mobility				
63	ONE LEG CIRCLE	Mobility	o	o	o	o
64	THE HUNDRED	Strength	o	o	o	o
66	THE SEAL	Mobility				
67	ONE LEG STRETCH	Strength				
68	THE SAW	Mobility	o	o	o	o
69	SHOULDER BRIDGE PREP	Mobility				
70	SIDE KICK	Strength				
71	SPINE STRETCH	Mobility	o	o	o	o
72	SPINE TWIST	Mobility				
74	THE CRAB	Mobility				
75	DOUBLE LEG STRETCH	Strength	o	o	o	o
76	ROCKER WITH OPEN LEGS	Mobility	o	o	o	o
77	SHOULDER BRIDGE	Strength	o	o	o	o
78	SIDE BEND	Strength	o	o	o	o
80	SIDE-KICK KNEELING	Strength	o	o	o	o
81	THE TEASER	Strength	o	o	o	o
82	JACK KNIFE	Strength	o	o	o	o
83	HIP TWIST	Strength			o	o
84	SCISSORS	Strength	o	o	o	o
85	THE ROCKER	Strength			o	o
86	THE BOOMERANG	Mobility	o	o	o	o
87	NECK PULL	Strength	o	o	o	o
88	CONTROL BALANCE	Strength				o
89	LEG PULL SUPINE	Strength		o	o	o
90	THE CORKSCREW	Strength			o	o
91	ROLLOVER	Strength	o	o	o	o

preventing pain

Pilates challenges us to examine how well our bodies are really functioning. Even the most healthy person may have niggling pains which indicate stresses and strains on the body. For others, the effects of ignoring the needs of our bodies is all too apparent. Pilates can help to build the body to prevent injury and help to keep us healthy through the development of good posture.

Most of us experience painful twinges in our bodies from time to time. These are little warning signals of trouble ahead. If we do not listen to our bodies, then the signals they give us can only become more insistent. Even those who are extremely fit, such as top athletes, can develop medical problems as a result of the body working in ways that are disharmonious. This is particularly true for golfers and tennis players who use one side of their bodies very differently from the other.

Muscle balance

Muscular stress is often hidden by groups of larger muscles that develop to protect weaker ones. This is the body's way of coping with a problem, but it is only ever short term. Pilates exercises will reveal the original source of the problem and address it directly. There are no short cuts to solving bad posture and back pain. For

example, supporting devices, such as corsets, simply do the work that the muscles should be doing for themselves. We need to train our bodies to break their recourse to sloppy habits and learn new coping methods.

Pain and gain

These changes may at first feel uncomfortable but it is important to distinguish between this normal level of discomfort and the discomfort caused through the injury or problem itself. There is always a certain amount of discomfort that arises during training, especially when it comes to stretching muscles that you may not have used in some time. When stretching, it is best to think of discomfort along a scale of one to 10. Mild stretches rank one to four. From five on, you will be increasingly challenging yourself. A strong stretch may elicit some pain. Be careful not to push too

far at the top end of the scale. If any pain is sudden or sharp you must stop immediately as this extreme should never be experienced. Only people who are very in tune with their bodies, such as dancers or sportspeople, work at the top end of the scale in order to push their performance levels to the limit. Pilates involves you finding out your own level of discomfort. Begin at the lower end of the scale, regardless of your overall level of fitness. I emphasise again that stretching exercises should be performed gradually. It is always better to build up slowly. Only in this way can you strike a balance between achievement and challenge. Never exercise when you are in chronic pain or when any of your muscles are inflamed. Remember to always seek medical advice for back problems as they can occur for a host of different reasons. Never self-diagnose.

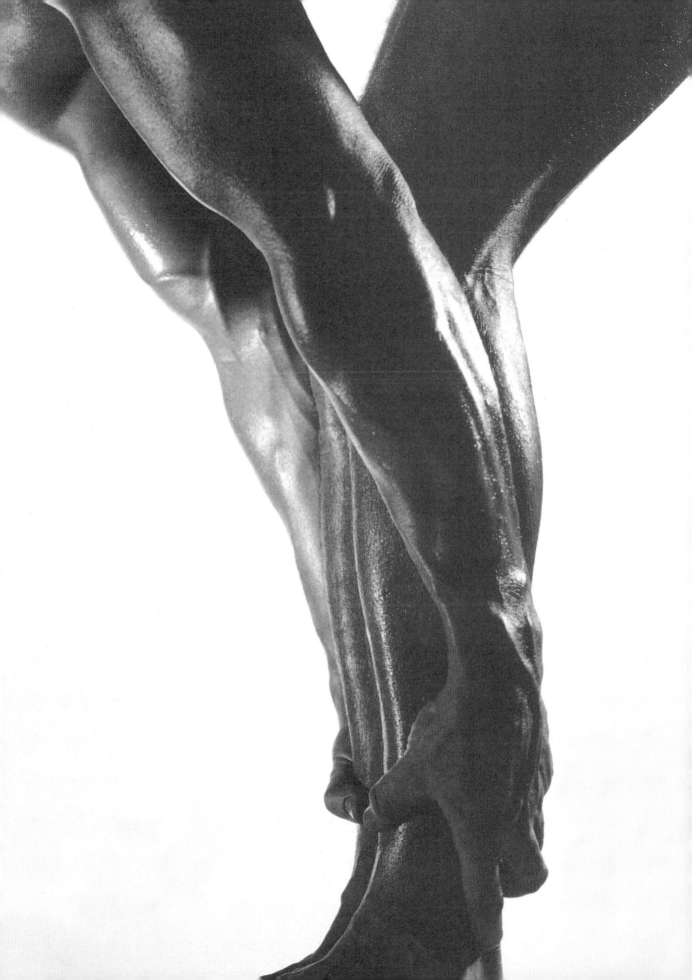

Your whole life

It is no good doing Pilates exercises for a few hours in the week if you spend the rest of your time slouched over a desk or slumped in front of the television. Pilates should make you think about the whole of your life and examine your everyday habits. Some of the suggestions set out here will complement your Pilates programme and ensure that the philosophy of balance and control behind Pilates extends into the rest of your life.

Correct posture

Our postural habits develop from the moment we learn to walk. How we live our lives affects our posture, and all too often this means adopting bad posture. To rectify this, Pilates movements return us to the floor once again. This helps to reduce the strain of gravity so that we can build our strength. Correcting bad posture takes time and patience but the rewards of doing so are multifold. Your posture can directly affect your health. Even small stresses and strains can add up over a period of years to cause serious, permanent damage. Your back always reflects what you do to it.

Back pain

In the industrial world, the most common health problem among those under 65 is back pain. It has been estimated that our bodies are not designed to be static for more than twenty minutes at any given time, yet our modern lifestyles often entail long periods of sitting down, especially at work. One of

the things Joseph Pilates noticed about animals, especially cats, was the way they were constantly stretching their limbs and muscles. He believed that this was one of the reasons they remained so supple, nimble and poised. In the same way, humans need to keep moving and stretching.

Developing spine

Babies are born with spines that are shaped like commas, with just one curve. But as we mature, our spines adopt an S-shape, with a hollow at the base of our necks and another in the small of our backs. Try to keep these natural curves in the course of everyday life, even while sitting down. Review the way your everyday activites may be leading to bad posture.If you slouch, your spines forms an unhealthy C-shape. You can take precautionary measures by adopting better postural habits.

In the office

Modern sedentary working conditions mean that the average office worker may spend between 25 and 40 hours a week sitting down in a chair. Add this to the time we spend sitting to eat at a table, driving a car or slumped in front of the television and you get a sense of just how vital good posture is in our daily lives. A comfortable office chair cannot in itself compensate for poor posture. It is important to try to sit as erect as possible for as long as you can. Your feet should always be kept flat on the floor and it is best not to sit with your legs crossed for long periods. If you

are working at a computer, it is best to look slightly down at the screen. Your forearms should be in a horizontal position. Make sure the back of your seat supports your lumber curve; a small cushion can help support the lower back. This doesn't mean you must sit like a tin soldier all of the time. Make sure you get up from your desk as often as you can. Try not to spend more than twenty minutes working in the same position. Walk around the room to stretch your spine and improve your circulation. Try to organise your day so that it includes a series of natural breaks.

At home

While at home we undertake activities that can lead to back pain though bad posture. All working surfaces should be at the correct height. Kitchen sinks, for example, are often too low. This means we may need to stoop uncomfortably over them , causing stress in our lower backs. If yours is like this, try to raise the bowl to ensure there is no need to stoop over it. If there's a cupboard underneath the sink, rest one foot on the lower shelf. Keep changing your feet on the shelf to maintain the natural balance of your back.

Couch potatoes

When you are watching television, try to get up off the sofa for a stretch every half an hour. Throw away the remote control and get to your feet! Many sofas are built too low for the average adult. You should be able to sit with your back against the sofa back and your feet on the floor. If the seat is too deep, pack the space behind your lumbar curve with cushions.

Lying down

Your bed can dramatically effect the health of your back. Poor beds can in themselves lead to back pain. A good bed should support your spine so that it is level. Your natural S-shape should be maintained while lying on your back. Yet the mattress should also mould to the contours of your body. Your mattress should be neither too hard nor too soft. You can test this by seeing whether you can fit your hand underneath the curve of your back. It should fit easily between bed and back, neither being squeezed too tightly nor having too much room. The term 'orthopaedic' is used by mattress manufacturers to sell their products although this can be misleading. It is best to choose a comfortable mattress that is right for just you, rather than one that feels extra hard.

Driving

When we drive our cars we are often confined in a small space for hours on end. Most people experience back pain after lengthy car journeys. There are steps you can take to avoid this. Make sure your driving position is as comfortable as possible and that the controls are within easy reach. Do not hunch over the steering wheel or slouch in the seat but sit in an upright position. Make sure your mirrors are correctly adjusted so that you don't have to strain. It is best not to grip the wheel too tightly as this will tense your muscles and add to stress. You could also try pulling in your stomach muscles and breathing out, or try raising your shoulders towards your ears and pushing your shoulders down against the back of the seat.

Back exercises

CORE WORK

All these Pilates movements will strengthen your core, building strength in the muscles that support your spine

The hundred (p64)

Roll-up (p60, 62)

Swimming (p56)

One leg stretch (p67)

The seal (p66)

Double leg stretch (p75)

Spine twist (p72)

OFFICE EXERCISE

• Pull in your chin, turn your head slowly to one side, without jerking it, before turning it to the opposite side. Repeat 3-4 times.
• Raise your shoulders up towards your ears then push them back and relax. Repeat 2-3 times.
• Tighten your abdominal muscles as you breathe out fully and count to five before releasing.
• When you are having a break from sitting down, stand with your feet apart and place your hands in the small of your back. Keeping your knees straight, push your hips forward and your shoulders back. This will release tension in the spine.

Avoiding back pain

PREVENTATIVE MEASURES

• Always aim to keep the normal S-shape curves of your spine in place for most of the day.
• Try to avoid hunching up your shoulders or slumping forward causing your spine to form an unhealthy C-shape.
• Take frequent breaks to move around as much as you can. Try not to remain in a single fixed position for more than 30 minutes.
• Tuck in your abs as much as you can, especially when lifting something.
• To pick up heavy objects, bend your knees and keep your back straight; never bend over. Try to keep objects near to your body as you pick them up.

TO REDUCE PAIN

• Try to keep up your normal daily activities. Gentle exercise will strengthen your back muscles and improve flexibility. Avoid strenuous exercise such as aerobics.
• Try to avoid lifting heavy weights. Make several short trips to the shop rather than trying to carry heavy groceries all in one go.
• When sitting, both your feet should be resting on the ground. Do not cross your legs.
• If, after a few days, your pain persists, visit a qualified manipulative therapist such as an osteopath, chiropractor or physiotherapist.

vital elements

concentration

With many exercise classes and techniques you don't have to think about what you're doing, you just do it to get through it. But with Pilates, every movement is a conscious act controlled by the power of your mind.

'Always keep your mind wholly concentrated on the purpose of the exercises as you perform them.' Joseph Pilates

Pilates is 'the thinking way of moving' and requires a different kind of concentration than that typically used for other exercise forms. It may not be all that important to concentrate in this way during an aerobics class or when walking on a treadmill, but it is absolutely essential for Pilates.

Setting the mood

There are simple things you can do to improve concentration. Check that the space you plan to use for Pilates is free of distractions and that it is warm and comfortable. Make sure you will not be disturbed. Though Pilates is not a spiritual workout, you will find it very relaxing because concentrating hard on a single movement causes everything else that is going on in your life to fade away. If you want to use music in the background, make sure it isn't punctuated by a heavy beat. Do not make the

mistake I once made when I used a tape of nature sounds that featured screeching parrots and mating whales!

A clear mind

You'll soon find that the benefits of practising concentration are well worth the effort – easier mental focus, clarity of thought and, most importantly, reduction of stress. All too often in our

whirlwind modern lives, visual clutter and noisy distractions make it hard for us to focus on the task at hand. Stress itself makes concentration more difficult (when you have too many things 'on your mind') but persevere, as mental focus is an art that will improve with practice. Marshalling your powers of concentration will help you to feel more calm and in control.

Our inner voice

Controlling our thoughts, much like controlling our actions, is not as easy as it might first appear to be. When we are under pressure, our thoughts can become very erratic and spin off in random directions. If we are stressed, going to sleep can be especially difficult because we are unable to 'switch off'. Unwelcome thoughts pop into our heads despite our best efforts.

Effective concentration is a skill we acquire as children. By the time we are adults, we all have a little 'inner voice' that controls our actions, for

example when we tell ourselves that we do like a particular exercise.

First attempts at unfamiliar movements may feel strange and awkward. It is very easy to fall into the trap of performing only the moves that you enjoy, when what you need most is to do the ones you do not like. Normally we speed up the difficult part of the movement to get it over with as soon as we can. Instead, we need to slow down. Only by concentrating hard on what you are doing can you properly control your actions.

breathing

Pilates uses a controlled and continuous way of breathing that takes time to perfect, but results in a stronger and more energy-efficient body.

'Breathing is the first act of life. Our very life depends on it. Millions have never learned to master the art of correct breathing.'

Joseph Pilates

Correct breathing takes time to master. Of all the vital elements, my students find this the most difficult to achieve and the last to fall into place. The main thing to remember is to breathe as frequently as you would naturally. If you find a movement is too slow for a single breath and you need to take another, take one.

Many Pilates instructors ask you to learn the breathing technique before learning the movements. My goal is the same, but my approach is different. I believe you can learn correct breathing while learning each of the movements.

The wrong way

Whatever you do, don't hold your breath. Most people hold their breath if they pick up something heavy, much as weightlifters would when picking up a barbell. This type of breathing is called the Valsalvic method and it results in a stressful increase in blood pressure. It wastes energy in parts of the body where it isn't required. Keep your breathing continuous.

Normal breathing

When you inhale normally, the lungs expand, the diaphragm drops and the stomach moves out. As you exhale, your diaphragm lifts and the stomach moves in. This is called 'abdominal' breathing and is quite natural.

Pilates breathing

For Pilates you need to learn a new breathing technique. To strengthen the abdominals they must be contracted. This means abdominal breathing is not possible. Instead we use thoracic breathing (see below). Imagine you are wearing an invisible belt that is pulling your bellybutton towards your spine. Squeeze the stomach and breathe into the ribs.

Thoracic breathing

Try this breathing exercise. Sit comfortably on a chair or on the floor, with your legs crossed. Place your hands behind your back, with palms facing out and fingers touching your ribcage. Keeping your abdominals contracted, breathe in and feel your ribcage expand against your hands. Breathe in for two counts and out for two counts, repeating this several times. Now slow your breathing down to four counts for each in and out breath. Repeat this longer breath several times. Finally, try breathing in for eight counts and then out again for an equal eight counts. Aim to keep the abdominals contracted while breathing and breathe into your ribcage, rather than your stomach, so that the ribs expand outwards.

Or try this: place your right hand, palm down, on the lower front portion of your ribcage. Breathe into the one hand for eight counts, feeling your chest expand. Breathe out for eight. Repeat several times, change hands and repeat on the other side of your ribcage. Return to these exercises whenever the need arises.

centering

The centre of your body is the centre of your power. The body should work in unison not as separate parts, with all movement stemming from your centre.

'Pilates develops the body uniformly, corrects wrong postures, restores physical vitality, invigorates the mind and elevates the spirit.' Joseph Pilates

Joseph Pilates believed that our abdominal muscles, now known as abs, function as the 'powerhouse' for the whole of the body. Your abs are your centre and they initiate every movement. To maintain a strong centre you need an equal balance of strength, between the abs and the back.

Core essentials

When doing regular sit-ups we often think of moving first, then of pulling in our abs. We 'crunch' these stomach muscles as we lift up. What we should actually be doing is contracting our muscles first and then moving our limbs. Ultimately every movement should be initiated by the contraction of your abs; whether you are lifting your arm or your leg, the movement starts here.

Think of a puppet. When you pull a string, its arm goes up. Your abdominals act as your 'string'. Strength flows outwards along your limbs from this pivotal middle junction. Strong abs are the key to your body working as a unit and will help to strengthen all your other muscle groups.

Good foundations

Start each warm-up with the 'Striking balance' exercise (below). You can also practise balancing correctly the next time you are waiting in a supermarket queue.

Your feet support your body most effectively when they lie directly under your hips so that you can balance evenly on the ball of each foot, the outside edge of the foot and the centre of your heel. Women who usually wear high heels tend to lean backwards to compensate for the shoes' forward pitch. Ideally you should not push too far forward from your heels or back from your toes.

Striking balance

Stand with your bare feet shoulder-width apart. Lift your toes as high as you can. Imagine a triangle between your big toe, little toe and heel. Place this imaginary triangle evenly on the ground, letting your toes drop and spread out. Open your shoulders, lengthen your spine and imagine a string, attached to the top of your head, pulling you up to the ceiling.

Pull in your abs and breathe out as you push up onto the balls of your feet. Stretch up, as tall as possible. Then slowly lower your heels. Make sure your toes stay relaxed and don't crunch up. When your heels just touch the ground, keep your body weight in that position. Your body is now centred.

It might feel like you are leaning forward. This is because we are so accustomed to putting our weight on our heels. If you could look sideways in a mirror you should be able to draw a straight line vertically from your shoulders to your hips to the middle of your feet. To maintain this posture you have to keep your abdominals contracted, which makes the body work harder.

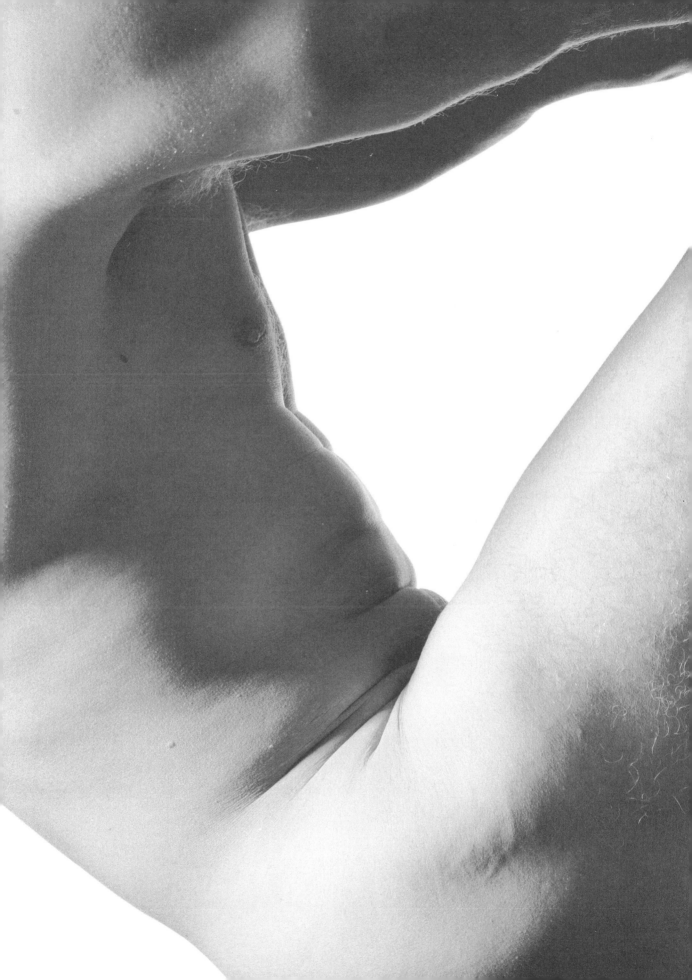

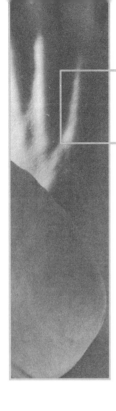

control

We start learning control when we take our first shaky steps as a child. Far from constricting us, good control frees our potential and teaches us how to take charge of our own bodies and fulfil our physical capabilities.

'Good posture can be successfully acquired only when the entire mechanism of the body is under perfect control.' Joseph Pilates

Imagine a child walking for the first time, staggering forward with arms stretched out. At this early age, on learning to walk, we are training our bodies to resist the pull of gravity. We begin developing strength and control and, as we get stronger, we walk with more skill. Over time our postural habits develop, but often not as they should. Through Pilates, we can go back a step and re-learn the art of control.

Go slow

All Pilates movements are slow and controlled. They should be done at the same constant speed throughout. None of the actions are jerky or frenetic as this puts your body at risk of injury. Slower movements are much harder to control and are, therefore, more exacting and ultimately more effective. Practising Pilates will show you how little you previously thought about your movements.

Perfect visuals

Imagine a man doing a bicep curl. His muscles are tense as he lifts the dumbbell, and then, quite often, the arm just relaxes and swings back down. If the down movement is uncontrolled, he only gains partial benefit from the workout. He also risks injury. In Pilates, control should be used at every point of the movement.

Think now of a gymnast standing on a narrow balance beam. She performs a forward roll and ends once again in a standing position. Her control and precision keep her from falling off, helping her to maintain a constant speed as she rolls. Visualising images can help you to understand control and maximise your workout. Use this image and work towards the same quality of movement in your Pilates. Try the 'Resist me' exercise (below) to see how effective visualisation can be.

Resist me

Find a partner. Stand up, holding a towel in your right hand. Have your partner sit down at your feet and hold the other end of the towel with both hands. Pull your fist, with the towel, towards your shoulder in a bicep curl. Let your partner create resistance so that there is equal tension as you move your arm up and down.

Think about a resistance scale from one to 10. One is when your partner exerts no resistance with the towel.

10 is when your partner pulls so hard that you can't move at all. Aim for a resistance level of five in both directions. Breathe out as you curl the arm up and breathe in as you uncurl the muscle. Repeat 10 times and change arms.

Next, drop the towel but imagine you are still holding it and repeat the bicep curl. Do you feel the resistance that you had when you were holding the towel? This visualisation technique will aid controlled action.

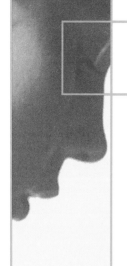

precision

Everybody has their own natural geometry. Pilates can help us to move with more precision and discover for ourselves the dimensions of natural grace.

'The benefits of Pilates depends solely on your performing the exercises exactly according to the instructions.'

Joseph Pilates

All Pilates movements are exact, and involve precise actions and precise breathing. When you think of precision and movement, you might think of synchronised swimmers or the exacting choreography that dancers can achieve. Remember that Joseph Pilates trained as both a boxer and an acrobatic circus performer. This gave him an appreciation of precision skills and an acute awareness of space and time.

Catching the moment

The most dramatic example of precision I have ever witnessed was the Cirque de Soleil show called 'O' in Las Vegas . The piece combines the precise acrobatic skills of the performers with advanced stage technology. Accuracy was vital in the performance, not just for effect but also for the safety of the performers. To my joy, as I looked through the programme of this incredible event, I saw that two full-time Pilates instructors were listed as staff members. This level of physical activity requires extreme concentration, but we can all practise precision to some degree through Pilates.

Perfect reach

Bring to mind the image of the spread-eagled figure drawn by Leonardo da Vinci. The artist has drawn a circle around the figure as he stretches out to his fullest extent. These lines of geometry are a useful visualisation of the space around us.

Usually we are unaware of the space we occupy and how our movements take place within it. Because Pilates demands that you not only move correctly, but breathe correctly, you will become more aware as to how your personal space is created through concentration and the use of precision. It is through precision

Spot on

My version of the popular game *Pin the Tail on the Donkey* requires no donkey and no pin. Just stand up and find a spot on the door in front of you. Slowly reach out with your right arm and touch the spot. As you bring your right arm back, begin stretching your left arm out to touch the same point. Repeat for 30 seconds, keeping the alternate movement of the two arms continuous. Do not stop and make sure the elbows do not lock.

Now turn around and imagine that same point but in an imaginary space in front of you. Focus on that spot and again reach for it with your right hand, alternating with your left hand, but without the help of the visual cue. Keep going for at least another 30 seconds, always aiming for the same point in space. You have just practised precision.

that we can attain grace of movement. Imagine the arm of a ballet dancer arching like the tip of a compass; we are all capable of making pin points in space.

movement

Think slow, controlled and continuous movements. Imagine a wheel turning slowly, never speeding up or slowing down, and never pausing.

'Designed to give you suppleness, grace, and skill that will be unmistakably reflected in the way you walk, the way you play, and in the way you work.' Joseph Pilates

When I explain to new students the type of movement required for Pilates exercises, I always compare it to tai chi. It is slow, graceful and controlled. As with tai chi, all Pilates movements are continuous: they have no beginning and no end. Nothing is sharp, strained or forced.

No sweat

With many exercise techniques the focus is on repetition and you stop after each one. Pilates movements are different in that you don't pause until you have completed the required number of repetitions. Each movement is a long, continuous cycle as this requires greater skill to control. If you need to be convinced that slow, controlled movements are more difficult, try the 'Slower is harder' challenge (right). The truth is that there is no need for you to work up a sweat or exercise at speed for it to be effective!

Full range

This type of movement can be applied to other forms of exercise with much success: try using resistance machines or free weights in the gym with slow, steady and even movements. You will be able to feel the difference and it will prove more effective (you may have to use a lighter weight). It is also vitally important to ensure that you are using your full range of movement. Check that you are working equally hard, with the same intensity and resistance throughout. As much effort should be used to extend a muscle (eccentric movement) as to contract it (concentric movement). By working in this way, you will begin to develop strength and flexibility in equal measure, giving your muscles (and your body) a long, lean look.

Slower is harder

Begin by doing five regular push-ups (press-ups), either with your legs fully extended in the full push-up position, or with your knees on the floor (the three-quarter position). Do these first five at your normal pace.

Now do another five, but count two slow counts down and two slow counts up. Breathe in as you go down and out as you come up. Rest. Now repeat, but to a count of four in each direction. Rest. Finally, try a last five push-ups, to a count of six on the way down and another six on the way up, without pausing at the top or at the bottom, making all five push-ups one long, continuous and steady movement. It was harder than you thought, wasn't it?

At this latter point you are working at the same intensity that you should be working at while doing the Pilates exercises. It is all about quality and range of movement, with the contraction of the muscles (the downward movement in this case) and the flexion (the pushing up movement) requiring equal effort.

isolation

The Pilates technique is an excellent way of educating yourself and understanding, through movement, how your body works, in part and as a whole. Harmony comes from the integration of isolated parts.

'Each muscle may cooperatively and loyally aid in the uniform development of all our muscles.' Joseph Pilates

For many years exercise teachers have talked about isolating different muscles. Yet it is only theoretically possible to see them in isolation; in practice, all our muscles work together in groups. Again, in regular exercise classes, we have also talked about 'spot reducing' certain areas to achieve a desired look. But in doing this we develop one muscle at the expense of another. Consequently, the whole balance of the body is thrown. This 'lopsided' approach is altogether at odds with the logic of the Pilates method.

Muscle balance

When we talk about isolation in Pilates we are simply making sure that we identify all our muscles for ourselves, especially the weaker ones. Pilates exercises ensure we develop the neglected areas of the body that work alongside opposing, stronger muscles. For example, if you are a golfer, you know that when you play you only swing in one direction. Over a period of time your body will become over-trained in this direction. Although we don't all play golf, we do all harbour muscle imbalances to some degree. It is not uncommon to discover these over- or under-trained areas through Pilates.

Weak links

Try to be aware of any imbalance in muscle strength or flexibility as you perform the movements and work towards the weaker of the two sets of muscles, so that balance is eventually regained. Otherwise, as you get stronger you will remain proportionally imbalanced. Try the 'Touch and visualise' exercise to better understand how muscles work. Learn to identify the location of, say, your tricep without actually having to touch it. Visualisation techniques will help you to

Touch and visualise

Sit down on a chair with a dumbbell, or bag of sugar or bottle of water to use as a weight. Sitting upright, hold the weight above your head in the right hand, with your right arm stretched straight towards the ceiling. Bring the left hand up to touch the back of your upper right arm with the tips of your fingers, keeping your right elbow close to your head. Lower the weight slightly behind your head and lift it back again to the ceiling. With the fingers of your left hand feel the tricep muscle at the back of the arm contracting and extending. Repeat 10–20 times. Now shift the weight to the other hand and repeat.

Finally, repeat the movement without the weight and without touching the triceps. Try and visualise the muscle working, from what you have just experienced.

connect mentally with the muscle. Over time you will be able to feel and identify various muscles working in combination as you perform the movements.

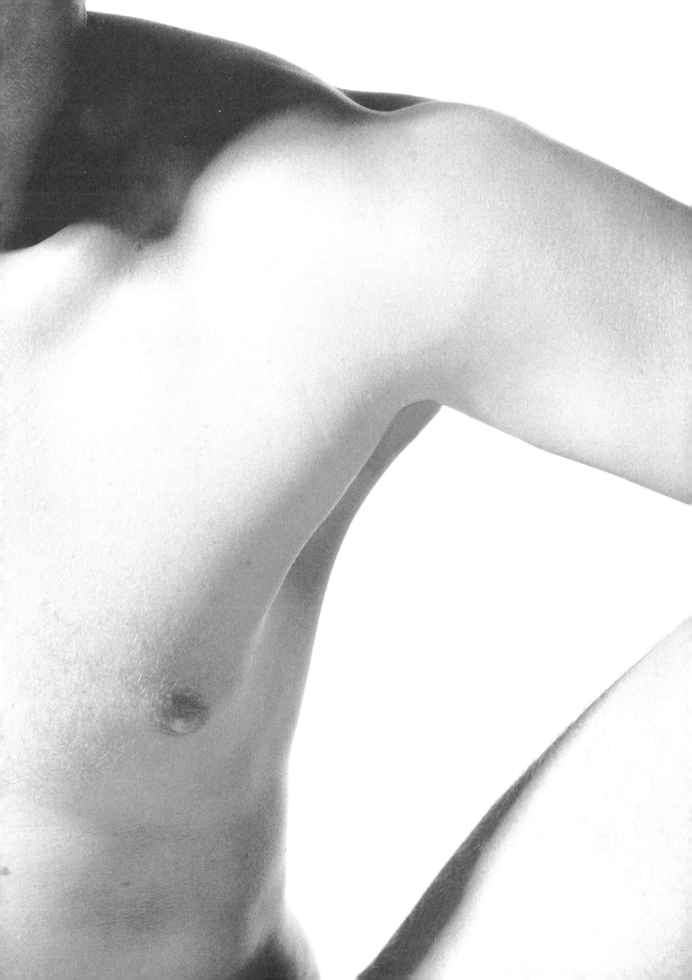

routine

Pilates is not an 'instead of' but an 'as well as' – it does not replace your current exercise programme, but rather compliments and enhances it by improving the way your muscles work together. But you must practise!

'Make up your mind that you will perform your Pilates movements 10 minutes [each day] without fail.' Joseph Pilates

The development of a routine will help you get the best from Pilates. It does not promise quick-fix solutions but it does achieve real results by offering a gentle overhaul of your daily habits.

Making time

I often hear people say 'I don't have time to exercise'. But I have found that the easiest way to help my clients develop a routine is for them to treat Pilates as an important business appointment. They schedule it into their diaries as they would any other meeting. Devoting thirty minutes every day to the maintenance of your body is scant attention, especially when you stop to consider what you ask your body to do for you. We often treat our cars with more care than we do our bodies. Yet there is no question of trading in your body for a new model! Sticking to a routine is a way of taking yourself and your body seriously.

Regular slots

People often ask me, 'How often should I do it?' and there is no easy answer. Like anything, the more you do it, the more quickly you will see results. Look at your goals and other commitments and decide how much time you can you can really dedicate to Pilates. Then be patient as you develop a regular routine. Bear in mind that Pilates in itself is not a

replacement for cardiovascular activities and should always be combined with a balanced workout programme. Gradually you will feel the muscles around your hips and waist tighten and tone as your body shape begins to change. Doing Pilates two or three times a week will also add to the effectiveness of other exercise programmes as it promotes strength, flexibility and balance.

Practise makes perfect

Many of my clients want to know when their bodies will begin to look different. I always say, 'If you've done the striking balance exercise, you will already look different. But maintaining good posture takes time.'

We want instant results but, as with everything else, progress takes time and practise. Think of it as being like learning to drive. We need to develop new skills, and the more lessons and experience we have, the better drivers we become. It is exactly the same with your body and Pilates.

When you practise this technique your muscles will become leaner through regular stretching. Pilates not only changes body shape but will also increase your body strength.

Although we often look for cosmetic results, Pilates places just as much importance on the fundamental realignment of our bodies that will make them more flexible and pain-free. This process is not a magical one but simply the logical result of training your body to behave in new and more balanced ways.

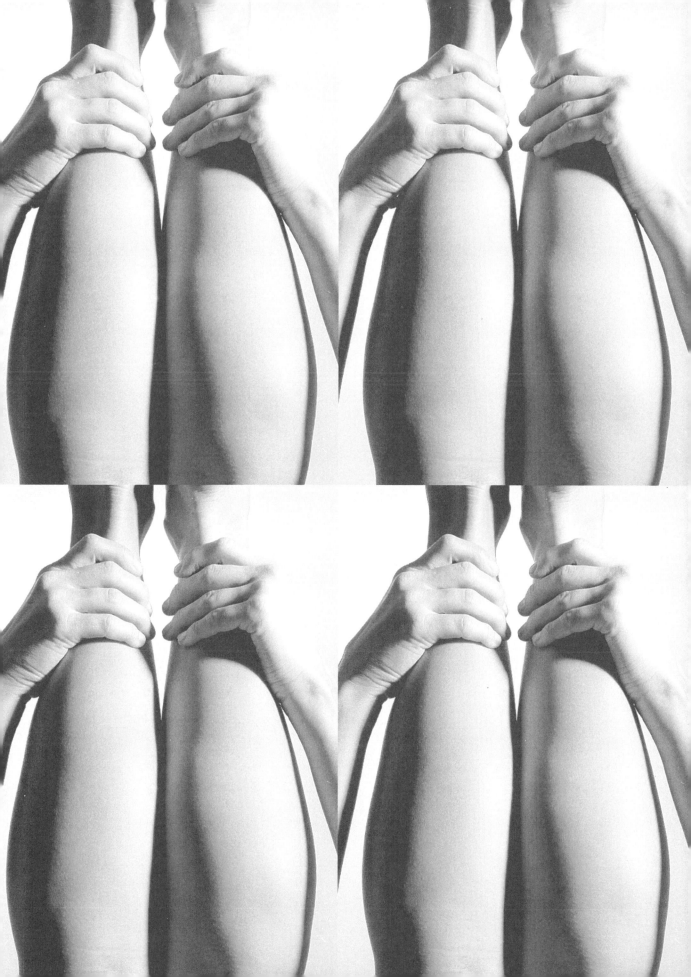

movements

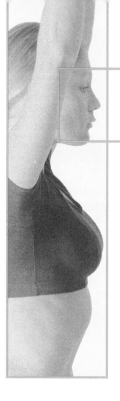

warm-ups

The warm-up is an essential part of your regular programme and should precede every session of Pilates. Warming up prepares your body for the movements ahead by improving the blood flow from your heart to your muscles. Use this time to concentrate on your body. Shut out the events of the day and focus on your posture and movements.

swinging

This movement will warm up your spine and back muscles. Be gentle with yourself and do not force the body. Move slowly and with control, as if you were moving through water.

emphasis	mobility
visual cue	low
	bow
repeat	20 times

1 With your feet apart and knees relaxed, stretch your arms up to the ceiling, but not past your head. Pull in your abs.

2 Breathe out and let your arms fall forward past your head. As they swing, allow your knees to bend and your back to curve. Relax your head and shoulders and pay attention to your spine as it gently relaxes, curling over. Keep your abs tight and the movement gentle.

3 After reaching the curled position, breathe in and roll slowly back up to the standing position. Each time you repeat the movement, try to stretch a little further towards the ceiling. Imagine a string is attached to the top of your head, pulling your entire body upwards.

round back

emphasis	mobility
visual cue	cat stretch
repeat	10 times

1 Put your hands on your thighs and lengthen your spine by stretching your head and neck diagonally upwards. Your tail bone should curl away from you. Pull in your abs and let your shoulder blades slide down your back.

2 Breathe out and gently round your back. Imagine a string attached to your waistband, pulling you up and backwards. Repeat the warm-up without stopping; keep working in a single continous movement. Breathe in as you return to the starting position and be sure to avoid hollowing your back in the opposite direction.

chest stretch

This movement warms up the chest muscles. Do not reach the same point each time but try and spread your arms further. Visualise that you are creating space in the joints.

emphasis	mobility
visual cue	cutting a 'V' shape
repeat	10 times

1 Stand tall with your feet apart, knees soft and your arms stretched out with palms up in front of you. Breathe in.

2 Breathe out and stretch your arms up and to the sides. Keep your spine long by pulling that invisible string to the ceiling. As you open your arms check that you are contracting your abs. Do not let your back arch. Keep the movement slow and the speed constant.

one arm circles

This movement opens up the shoulder joints.

❗ CAUTION

Do not lock your elbows and always work within your limits. If you find that you are able to make bigger circles on one side than the other then work on the weaker side in order to achieve balance in the body.

emphasis	mobility
visual cue	drawing circles
repeat	10 times

1 Stand tall with your feet apart, knees soft. Reach up from the top of your head to the ceiling to check that your back is correctly aligned. Keeping your right arm by your side, pressed lightly against the leg, breathe in and lift your left arm in front of you and slightly to the side.

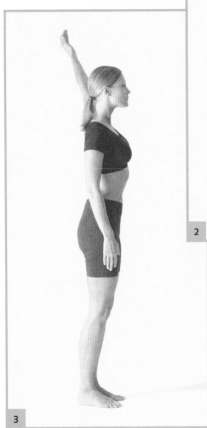

2 Keeping the ribcage still, start to draw a circle with the arm as you breathe out. If the ribcage moves, you are swinging too far – move the arm further away from the body to the side and draw a smaller circle. Imagine you are drawing on the wall to the side of you with the tips of your fingers.

3 Complete the circle, trying at all times to keep a slow, consistent speed. Imagine a wheel turning, where the motion is continuous and there are no sudden jolts. When you have completed 10 circles on one arm, change arms and repeat.

double arm circles

emphasis	mobility
visual cue	arm hoops
repeat	10 times

1 Stand tall with your feet apart, knees soft. Start with your arms slightly in front of you. Keep your abs pulled in and check that your back is in alignment.

2 Breathe out slowly and circle both arms back. Try to keep your hands together as you reach to the ceiling. Check your back does not arch by keeping your abs pulled in as tightly as possible.

3 Keep the speed of your movement constant and try to increase the size of the circle. When you reach 10, repeat in the opposite direction.

toy soldier

emphasis	mobility
visual cue	air paddle
repeat	10 times

1 Stand tall with your feet apart and knees soft. Breathe in. Reach your left arm to the ceiling and your right arm to the ground.

2 Breath out as you bring the lifted arm forwards and down, swapping to lift the lower arm up to the ceiling. Keep your torso still and stretch the top of your head to the ceiling. Keep the speed slow and the action smooth. Repeat 10 times.

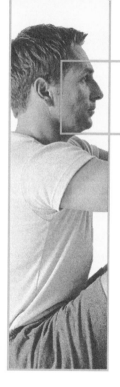

the essentials

The following movements are the building blocks of the Pilates technique. As always, start with the easier alternatives and work your way up to the pure version of the movement. Take time to work through each exercise. Listen to your body – you should never struggle to complete any of the movements. It is always best to develop strength slowly but surely.

push-up

Think of this as one long and continous slow movement. The speed is very important. Try slowing down the movement each time in order to challenge yourself.

■CAUTION

Find out where you need to put your hands in order to maintain control.

emphasis	strength
visual cue	snail on a wall
repeat	10 times

1 Stand tall with your feet apart, knees soft. Breathe in and contract your abs as you prepare to start slowly rolling your head and trunk down.

2 If you know you have a tightness in a certain area of your back, slow down as you pass through that area. Keep your abs pulled in. Imagine you are leaning against a wall so that your bottom does not push back. It should feel as though you are folding in on yourself.

3 As you roll down, try to go as far as you can without forcing the stretch. If you feel any uncomfortable strain on your back, bend your knees slightly to release stress in your back.

4 If you cannot touch the floor at the furthest point of your roll down, bend your knees and lean forwards. On contact, breathe out and walk your hands forward on the floor.

5 Keep the movement slow, smooth and gentle, as though you are trying to be silent.

6 Stop walking when your hands are at shoulder level. Stretch longer by sliding your shoulders down your back, keeping your body straight.

7 Breathe in and bend your arms to lower your chest towards the floor. Breathe out as you push back up and then walk your arms back and uncurl, reversing steps 6 to 1.

push-up alternative

If this movement at first proves too challenging, and you cannot complete a full stretch push-up, then drop to your knees for positions 6 and 7. The closer your hands are to the legs the easier the push-up will be. As your strength builds, work up to the straight leg version.

swimming

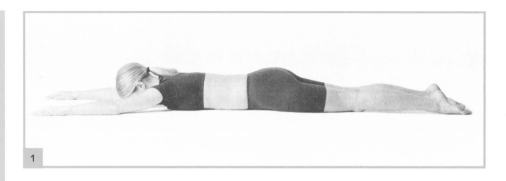

1 Lying face down, stretch the top of your head forward and slide your shoulders down your back. Stretch your legs behind you keeping them hip-width apart and contract your abs to lift your navel off the floor. This is the position you must try to maintain throughout the movement.

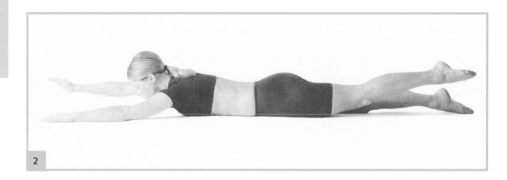

2 Breathe out as you lift your left leg and right arm up and away from you. Lift your limbs as high as you can without touching the mat with your navel. Feel your muscles lengthening along the floor before you lift. Do not struggle to lift too high as the lengthening is more important.

3 Breathing in, lower the limbs to change to the other side. Your little finger and little toe should be on the same diagonal line in space. Keep the movement slow and controlled. The speed of the movement should stay the same on both the lifting and the lowering of your limbs.

swimming alternatives

Try these easier alternatives if you feel any stress or pain in the lower back. Instead of lifting your abs keep them on the ground. This will limit the scope of the movement. Focus on your centre and not your legs as you move. Work towards lifting your abs by visualising that the floor is hot and that you do not want to burn your navel.

The aim is always to maintain a neutral spine in a face-down position (see page 73 for a description of the neutral spine). As this movement is hard to achieve for some, you may find yourself crossing the line from control to struggle. Avoid this by taking your time. Push your legs and arms into the floor before you try to lift them.

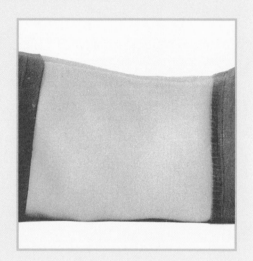

1 Isolate the upper body by keeping both legs down. Breathe out as you lift your head and right arm up and away from the floor. Breathe in as you lower your arm and swap to the left. Your goal is to keep your navel off the mat.

2 Isolate the lower body by putting your head on your arms in front of you. Slide your shoulders down your back. Breathe out as you lift the right leg away from you. Tighten the stomach and lift off the floor. Lower the right leg and change to the left.

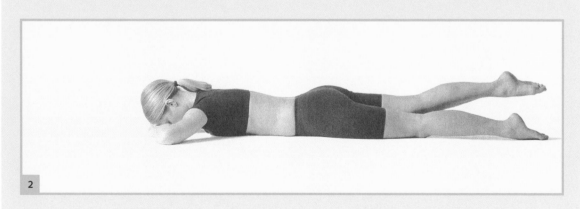

leg pull prone

emphasis	strength
visual cue	coffee
	table
repeat	10 times

1 Start in a push-up position with your back in a straight line and your abs tucked in so as to protect your back. Be sure not to let your bottom lift higher than your shoulders. Keep your shoulders pulled down and held in place and do not lock your elbows. Breathe in.

2 Breathe out as you raise your left leg, not letting your hips move. Initiate the lift by contracting your abs. Pretend you are a puppet: when you pull the string of the puppet the leg lifts. Your string is your abs being tightened.

3 Breathe in as you lower the leg and breathe out as you change to lift up the other leg. Your goal should be to ensure that your hips do not move. Keep your back straight. Check that your shoulders are pulled down your back and that your neck is stretched. Legs should be lifted and lowered slowly and continuously, with no change in speed.

leg pull prone alternatives

ALTERNATIVE 1

Rest your forearms on the ground, placing them as wide apart as your shoulders. Because you are now nearer the floor, the pull of gravity is less and you will find the leg moves easier to control. Try to keep your balance and keep the motion smooth.

1

ALTERNATIVE 2

1 If the leg lifting proves too difficult at first, try practising your balance by holding this position. Place your forearms firmly on the floor and curl your toes. Toes and hands should be aligned.

1

2 For a less intense version, place your knees on the ground also. Remember to keep your abs tucked in and hold your bottom down in line with your shoulders.

2

3 To reduce the intensity even further, lower the hips down. You should be resting the weight of your lower body on both of your feet. Tuck in your abs and feel your weight shifting as you push down on your arms.

3

roll-up

This movement is intended to develop your abdominal strength.

▌ CAUTION

If it proves too difficult to roll up off the floor then you will need to focus more on the mobility of your back. Do not attempt to force this move or struggle to complete it.

emphasis	strength
visual cue	rising sun
repeat	10 times

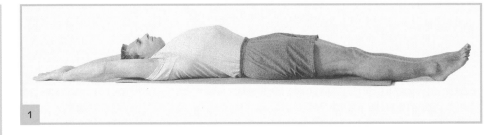

1 Lie on the floor on your back with your legs straight and stretch your arms above your head. Check that your shoulders are pulled down your back.

2 Slowly lift your arms to the ceiling as you breathe in. Try to keep a neutral spine (see page 73 for description of this) as your arms lift up.

3 Breathe out and slowly roll forward, peeling your spine off the mat. Keep your head in alignment and let your eyes lead the way. Keep your trunk taught and do not crunch the body.

4 Stretch out over your legs as you breathe in, then slowly roll back down to the floor as you breathe out. Do not pause but continue to roll up again, each time trying to reach a little further towards your toes.

roll-up alternatives

This variation allows you to start at a lower level as your strength builds and the flexibility in your back improves. You will be able to stretch a little further every time you return to this movement. Remember to keep your feet firmly set on the floor at all times.

1 Start from a seated position with your arms stretched out in front of you. Sit tall as if you have a hook at the top of the head which is pulling you up towards the ceiling. Slide your shoulders down your back and position your legs with knees bent, at a comfortable distance from your body. You should be able to sit without hunching your shoulders.

2 Breathe in and roll back to the point where you feel you can still keep control of the movement. This will be determined by the flexibility of your back and the strength in your centre. Breathe out on your return to the seated position. Do not stop at this point. Keep moving and complete 10 movements. As you become more flexible you will be able to lean further back.

listen to your body

Our bodies are never the same day-to-day and so you should expect your capabilities to vary. Working out on a Friday, after a long week, will feel very different from exercising on a Monday morning after a full weekend of rest. Proper rest is sometimes the only cure for fatigue. According to recent research, the average person sleeps about two hours less per night than he or she did twenty years ago. Sound sleep is essential for effective exercise. Your body and its metabolism will also vary with the seasons. In winter, it takes more time to warm up the body whereas in the summer our bodies remain at higher temperatures. Eating habits also come into play. I find that my body behaves very differently after lunch. Joseph Pilates compared heavy eating immediately followed by sitting or lying down, as 'overloading the firebox with coal and then closing the drafts to the furnace'. In contrast, food is the fuel of your body and if your tank is empty you may find your performance suffers. Joseph suggested we expend our energies in proportion to the amount of fuel we consume. Balance is the key.

rolling back

1 Sitting tall, lift from your centre, imagining a taut string connecting the crown of your head to the ceiling. Bend your legs and place your feet together, flat on the floor. Place your hands on your shins and pull in your stomach muscles.

2 Taking a slow breath in, curl your pelvis and start the roll, with your chin near your chest and spine curled.

3 Gently roll back only as far as your shoulders. As you roll back up, with abs still contracted, begin to breathe out slowly. Complete the breath as you return to the seated position and lengthen your spine to the ceiling. Aim to make the roll as smooth as possible.

rolling back alternative

1 If you can't manage the above without straining, try this easier alternative. Use your hands as supports with palms down and close behind you.

2 Breathe in as you tilt the pelvis and roll back, using your arms to support your weight as much as needed while you roll up again.

one leg circle

This movement opens up the hip joint, increasing mobility.

❚ CAUTION

If your hips move, you are taking the rotation too wide. You may find that each side has a different range of mobility. Limit your movement to the range allowed by the least flexible hip and keep the leg motion smooth. This will eventually restore balance to both hips.

emphasis	mobility
visual cue	clock
repeat	10 per leg

1 Lie relaxed and flat on the mat with your arms at your sides and palms down. Pull in your abs. Pointing your toes, stretch the left leg to the ceiling as far as possible without straining. Maintain a neutral spine (page 73).

2 Rotate the left leg clockwise, using the hip joint as the centre of the clock face. Always breathe in from 12 to six o'clock and breathe out from six to 12 o'clock. Repeat anti-clockwise and then switch to your right leg.

one leg circle alternatives

ALTERNATIVE 1

Keep one leg bent at the knee, foot flat on the floor, to stabilize the body. This will decrease the range of rotation for the raised leg and make it easier to maintain a neutral spine. It may also help to imagine you are drawing a circle on the ceiling with your big toe. Breathe in and out, using the same clockwise rotation practised in the previous movements.

ALTERNATIVE 2

This time lower the raised leg to a 90° angle and draw the circle of the clock with your knee, stretching up from the hip.

the hundred

The hundred is used to strengthen the torso. You are challenging yourself to keep a neutral spine while counting to a hundred. Use your arms to count the rhythm and breathe in for five counts and out for five counts. Find a position which allows you to keep a neutral spine.

emphasis	strength
visual cue	steep slope
repeat	10 times

THE ESSENTIALS

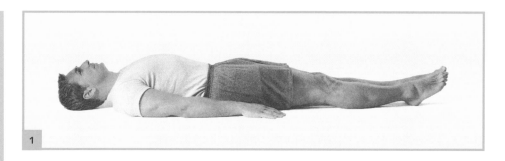

1 Lie on your back and check that your spine is neutral (page 73). Point your feet and lengthen your spine by pushing the top of your head away from you. Your shoulders should be pulled down your back.

2 Lift both legs up to a height where you are still able to maintain a neutral spine. At the same time lift your head up off the floor. Imagine you are holding an orange under your chin.

3 With a small movement, lift and lower your straight arms about two inches off the floor and breathe in for five up-and-down beats and out for five beats. Repeat this ten times until you have completed a hundred beats.

the hundred alternatives

! CAUTION

Maintaining neutral spine is not easy. It requires your back muscles to work in synergy with your abdominal muscles. It takes time to build strength and if you feel you are straining your back at any point then let it relax on the floor.

1 Lower the intensity of the exercise by bending the knees, so shortening the weight you have to hold up. Remember, the longer your legs are stretched the more weight you must bear.

1

2 To further decrease the intensity and the weight lift, place the right leg on the floor for 50 counts and change to the left leg for the remaining 50 counts. Work between the variations to feel the difference on both sides of the body.

2

3 With both legs on the ground you have no weight to bear except that on your upper body. Try to maintain this position, always remembering that a neutral spine (see page 73) is your goal.

3

4 Keeping your head and shoulders down, maintain neutral spine as you breathe in for five counts and out for five. Do this 10 times. Use your arms to count the beats. If you want to start with two sets of 50 and then build to 100, keep your spine long and keep your shoulders pulled down your back.

4

the seal

The second in the series of rolling exercises, this movement is used to create mobility and flexibility in the spine.

! CAUTION

If you find this too difficult, return to the basic rolling exercises where you may use your arms to support yourself.

emphasis	mobility
visual cue	rolling ball
repeat	10 times

1 Take a balanced position holding your legs lightly. Lift the top of your head to the ceiling and contract your abs.

2 Breathe in as you roll back onto your shoulders. Stay in a tight ball. As you roll, imagine that you are imprinting your spine into the mat.

3 Breathe out as you come back up and return the roll to the seated position. Use the muscles at your centre to power yourself back into the balanced position.

4 At the balanced position, lift the top of your head to the ceiling and gently pull your legs apart and push them together in three beats. Check that your spine is as straight as possible.

5 This beating of the feet adds to the balance period and also increases the strengthening element of the movement. Focus on your centre and imagine it is initiating the pull. The strength for the balance position should also come from your centre.

THE ESSENTIALS

one leg stretch

This movement challenges you to maintain a neutral spine while changing legs.

❚ CAUTION

Don't straighten the arm so far that the elbow joint locks. Avoid hunching your shoulders. There should be no pressure in the lower back.

emphasis	strength
visual cue	toe
	reach
repeat	10 times

1 Lifting your head and shoulders, hold your right leg gently and stretch the left leg away from you. The height of the leg is determined by the weight of your leg and the strength in your abs. Lift it higher if you feel your back arching.

2 Slowly swap to the other leg. Keep the movement continuous and breathe in for two changes and breathe out for two changes. Keep your elbows lifted and your head in alignment. If you feel any stress in the neck, put your head and shoulders down.

one leg stretch alternatives

1 You can further decrease the intensity of this movement by lowering one leg to the floor and keeping your head and shoulders down. Hold your knee gently and check that your back is in neutral position (see page 73).

2 As you stretch your leg away from you, breathe out. Breathe in as it retracts towards your centre. Try to ensure that your arms and legs are parallel and at the same angle. Repeat five times and then repeat with the other leg.

the saw

This movement works on the mobility and stretch of your upper back.

CAUTION

Do not force the stretch. Take it to the point of tension and relax to allow the final push. Do not struggle to complete the move. If touching your toes proves difficult, build up to it slowly.

emphasis	mobility
visual cue	plane
	propellor
repeat	10 times

1 Sit with your legs hip-width apart and your feet flexed. Lift your arms either side of you. They should not be open too wide, just enough so that you can see them as you look forward. Lift your head up as though you are in a cinema and trying to see over someone tall.

2 Breathe out and turn your body to the side. Keep your arms in line with your shoulders as you turn. Do not let them cross the body. Turn equally to the back and side keeping your hips facing firmly to the front.

3 Continue to breathe out as you stretch over your leg to the point of tension. Imagine you have a large beach ball over your knee and that you are stretching over it. Keep your head down as you stretch. Breathe in as you come back to the centre and repeat in the opposite direction on the other side.

shoulder bridge preparation

This movement is for opening and mobilising the whole spine.

▮ CAUTION

Do not force this movement. Be very gentle with your spine. If you know you have a tightness in a certain area, then slow right down as you pass through it. Concentrate on gently coaxing your muscles into becoming flexible.

emphasis	mobility
visual cue	ski slope
repeat	10 times

1 Lie on your back with your arms by your side. Think of the top of your head pulling you to one end of the room and your tailbone stretching to the other. Breathe in as a preparation, keeping your centre strong.

2 Breathe out and start rolling up towards the ceiling leading with your tailbone, letting your vertebrae lift one by one from the mat. Lift your hips up taking them to the height where your body forms a slope, no higher.

3 At the top of the movement stretch your arms behind you and breathe in. As you breathe out start rolling down back to the mat as if laying a string of pearls on a piece of velvet. Visualise each vertebra as it touches the mat.

side kick

This is a stretch move that challenges you to keep your balance as you take your leg forward.

■ CAUTION

Keep your shoulders stretched and do not allow your upper arm to move back. Do not lift your leg so far that you begin to lose your balance.

emphasis	strength
visual cue	side
	leap
repeat	10 times

1 Lie on your side and check that your spine is in a horizontal line. Pull in your abs. Your hips should be stacked one on top of each other. Stretch your legs as you also pull your upper body away from your centre.

2 Breathe out as you bring the top leg forward and breathe in as you slowly take it back. Find the range to keep control. Your strength is your centre and your body works as a whole. Repeat on the other side.

side kick alternatives

1 To reduce the balance and lower the intensity of this movement, lie down on your arm and place your upper arm in front of you. Check that your body is straight.

2 To further decrease the intensity of the movement, lift your torso on your elbow and place your upper arm behind your head. Check that you are lifting up off the floor with your upper body. You should feel no stress in your shoulders as you do this.

spine stretch

This movement is designed to help spine mobility.

⚠ CAUTION

If you cannot sit in a straight position, then try the easier alternatives. You can always place a towel underneath your bottom to raise your body at an angle that will help you to stretch your back.

emphasis	mobility
visual cue	beach ball
repeat	10 times

1 Sit with your legs in front of you and apart, your hands on the floor between them. Flex your feet and pull up from your abs, lifting your head to the ceiling. Keep extending yourself. Do not reach the same point as you come up but try to accomplish a higher point. Also think about your shoulders stretching to the sides, as if opening up the body wider.

1

2

2 Breathe out as you round your back and stretch forward. Try imagining you are stretching over a large beach ball. Take it to the point of tension and then roll back up, stacking the vertebrae one by one. Do not stop at any point in this movement but keep it free and flowing.

spine stretch alternative

If your back or hamstrings are tight then try this less intense variation.

⚠ CAUTION

Tight hamstrings should be stretched prior to this movement. Lean forward and hold a static stretch for a whole minute. Do not bounce.

Bend your knees and lift your toes then carry out the movement described above. If your arms get tired, you can bend the arms to a Cossack position and let your hands touch your shoulders. Stretch your spine from the base, tilting from the floor. Try not to curl your back or crunch over your abs.

spine twist

1 Sit with your legs apart and your arms stretched out wide to the sides. Do not extend your arms too far, they should rest at right angles to your outstretched legs. Now pull in your abs and straighten and lift your head. Imagine, once again, that a hook at the top of your head is pulling you to the ceiling.

1

2

2 Breathe out as you turn to the side, keeping your head reaching to the ceiling and your hips facing to the front. When you reach the point of tension, try to relax the body a little further.

3 Breathe in as you come to the centre and breathe out as you repeat the movement to the other side. Keep trying to take it a little further each time without forcing anything. If your arms get tired, you can use the Cossack arm position or bend your elbows so that your hands touch your shoulders.

3

THE ESSENTIALS

spine twist alternative

Sit with your knees bent, feet touching. Your legs do not have to have to be held too closely together. If you feel them tensing, push them further away in front of you. Now do the exercise described left. Sitting on a book or towel will help you to straighten out and sit up properly.

neutral spine

Many of the Pilates movements require you to maintain a 'neutral spine'. This is simply a term used to describe the natural curvature of your backbone. We all have three curves in our spine, the cervical (neck), the thoracic (upper back) and the lumbar (lower back). A correctly positioned spine should be S-shaped (although in reality the shape of your spine will be much softer and less pronounced than the curly letter S might imply). Bad posture makes us slump forward to form a C-shape.

Supine position

Explaining the idea of neutral spine is not always easy as it is not a fixed position. In order to find your own natural position try this easy exercise. Lie on your back on the floor with your

knees bent. Gently push your back down to touch the floor (in aerobics this used to be called a 'flat back'). If you were to stand up with your spine in this position you would be stooping over. Now take the body to the other end of the spectrum and gently arch your back. The neutral position is measured about half way between these

two extremes. Simply let your back relax into its normal 'supine' shape. Do not push your feet on the floor or tilt your pelvis up. Now put your hand under your back. You will find a space there. For some of us it is large and for others it is small. Everyone has a slightly different neutral position because we all come in slightly different shapes and sizes.

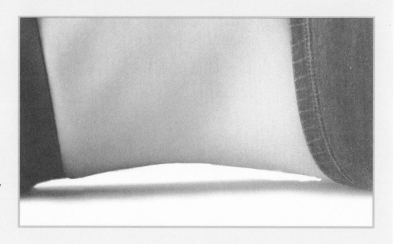

new challenges

After mastering some of the essential movements, try these more challenging and progressive ones. Listen to what your body tells you and only add them to your programme when you feel ready and able. It is fine to challenge yourself but do not exceed the comfortable range of movement or try so hard that you lose control and begin to struggle.

the crab

Like all the rolling movements, the crab uses your body weight to stretch the spine. Aim to slow the movement down until it can be completed with control of your abdominals.

⏸ CAUTION

Don't be surprised if you roll off to one side initially. This will decrease with time and practise.

emphasis	mobility
visual cue	crab
repeat	10 times

1 Use the same starting position as in rolling back (page 62). Cross your feet in front of you maintaining balance. Contracting your abs, lift your feet off the mat. Bring your arms around the legs and gently grasp the left foot with the right hand and the right foot with the left hand. Lift the feet slightly up towards your chest.

2 Initiate the roll by tilting the pelvis backwards. Breathe in on the roll down. Breathe out on the roll up, as you lengthen your body out. Remember to roll back only as far as your shoulders and to maintain control throughout. If this is hard, return to the seal.

double leg stretch

This movement is used to strengthen your abdominals and lower back. The weight of your legs and large circular motion of your arms challenge you to maintain a neutral spine throughout.

❗ CAUTION

If you begin to shake or are unable to maintain a neutral spine, raise your legs higher and decrease your arm movements. Otherwise try the alternatives below.

emphasis	strength
visual cue	morning stretch
repeat	10 times

1 Lay flat on the mat, contract your abs and maintain a neutral spine. Bring your knees in to your chest and place your hands on them.

2 Breathe in, straighten your legs and arms to a 45° angle and raise your head and shoulders off the mat. Keep your chin and head in line with your arms and legs.

3 Without moving your legs, start the large continuous arm circles by stretching your arms back over your head to your ears.

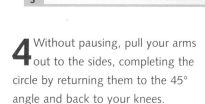

4 Without pausing, pull your arms out to the sides, completing the circle by returning them to the 45° angle and back to your knees.

double leg stretch alternatives

These easier alternatives provide greater stability and allow a wider range of movement with the arms.

❗ CAUTION

If you continue to experience strain in these two positions, simply keep both knees bent and feet flat on the floor for the time being.

ALTERNATIVE 1
Take some strain off your lower back by bending one leg and placing your foot flat on the mat.

ALTERNATIVE 2
If you feel strain in your neck and shoulders, keep them on the mat while completing the arm circle.

rocker with open legs

This movement works on the mobility of the spine. With the legs lifted you are also building up your strength.

❚ CAUTION

If you find the leg position in this movement too hard, try less intense movements such as basic rolling (p62) or the seal (p66).

emphasis	mobility
visual cue	rocking chair
repeat	10 times

1 Sit with your legs in front of you, knees up and slightly apart. Lift up your head as though it is strung to the ceiling. Pull in your abs. Open your shoulders, rolling them well down your back.

2 Hold your ankles and lift your legs to a balanced position. Push your legs away from you as you lift your head to maintain a long spine.

3 Keeping your balance, reach your legs out in front of you. The further you extend your legs the more you need to pull in your abs to maintain balance.

4 Breathe in as you roll back, keeping your legs the same distance from your body. Breathe out as you return to the balance position. Bend your knees slightly so you can touch your toes.

shoulder bridge

emphasis	strength
visual cue	ship's mast
repeat	10 times

1 Lie on your back with your knees bent and feet hip-width apart. Stretch your arms down by your side and stretch your spine back to reach your ears.

2 Breathe in as you roll your hips to the ceiling, peeling your spine from the mat vertebra by vertebra. Keep your abs pulled in. Only roll up as far as your shoulders.

3 Breathe out as you unfold your left leg to the ceiling, keeping your hips at the same height and not allowing them to drop. Use the strength in your centre to hold you in place.

4 Breathe in as you bring your leg down again, pointing your toe away from you.

5 Try to touch the floor as you stretch the leg down, breathing out as you lift the leg back to the ceiling. Breathe in as it touches the floor and then slowly breathe out as you roll the spine back down, laying the vertebrae back onto the mat one by one.

side bend

This movement builds strength as it challenges you to lift your body weight off the floor.

⚠ CAUTION

Pressure against a joint is good as it squeezes out all the old synovial fluid and draws in new fluid. But if you feel pressure at your elbow or wrist, try the alternatives.

emphasis	strength
visual cue	leaning tower
repeat	10 times

NEW CHALLENGES

1 Sit on your right hip with your arm straight and your hand under your shoulder. Bend your left leg and place it in front of your right leg, which should be straight. Pull up your head and tuck in your abs. Try to keep your hips forward so they are stacked one on top of the other.

2 Breathe out as you push on your left foot and start lifting your body to the ceiling. Reach out and up to the ceiling as your left arm draws a semi-circle through the air along your side. Your strength is in your centre which pulls in to create the movement. Keep your spine long as you begin to lift.

3 Continue to stretch until you are fully extended. Breathe in as you slowly lower your body back to the starting positon. Keep your speed the same as you are moving up and when you are coming down. Try to support yourself and keep your weight steady between each movement until you have completed the 10 repetitions. Repeat on the other side.

side bend alternatives

By lowering the movement you lower the degree of control needed to balance correctly.

! CAUTION

Keep your ribcage lifted up and don't let your shoulders sink. Don't place your weight onto your shoulders only.

ALTERNATIVE 1

1 Rest your body on your elbow, letting your hand reach forward in front of you. Lift your hand behind your head. Keep your abs tight.

2 Push up as you breathe out and lift your hip to the ceiling. Keep your hips stacked and try not to let them move or roll forward.

Lower the intensity by keeping your hand on the floor. and bending both knees.

! CAUTION

Keep any tension out of the region of your shoulders by sliding them down your back and mentally pinning them in place.

ALTERNATIVE 2

1 Keep your left hand on the floor as you rest on your right elbow. Bend both knees, keeping your knees and feet on top of each other. Don't let your hips roll forward.

2 Breathe out as you lift your hips up off the floor and only lift them to a height where you can keep control. Breathe in as you lower yourself back down.

side-kick kneeling

This movement is designed for strength. It challenges you to keep your torso in a neutral position as you use the weight of the leg swinging forward for balance.

! CAUTION

Do not try this if you have any history of problems with your knees.

emphasis	strength
visual cue	balancing scales
repeat	10 times

1 Kneel with your legs slightly apart and your arms stretched down by your side. Check that you are balanced in the centre and your pelvis is relaxed in neutral. Lift your head and pull up on your abs, checking your back is still in neutral position.

2 Move your weight out onto your right arm and make sure that you are evenly balanced on your arm and right leg. Point your toe and stretch the leg away from you, stretching your ears away in the opposite direction.

3 Pulling in your abs, lift your leg to hip height.

4 Keep your back in its neutral position, breathing out and bring your leg forward at hip height. Your goal is to keep your back still as you move your leg. Breathe in as your leg comes back to align with your hip. Repeat on the other side.

NEW CHALLENGES

the teaser

This movement is designed to increase strength. You challenge the body by lifting the torso up to a balanced position.

! CAUTION

The degree of intensity entailed in this movement can be decreased by keeping one leg on the floor at all times.

emphasis	strength
visual cue	horizontal dive
repeat	10 times

1 Sit with your knees bent in front of you and hold your legs lightly. Pull up on your centre as you straighten your head and pull yourself up towards the ceiling.

2 Breathe in and extend your legs, keeping a balanced position. Slowly lift your hands up towards your feet. Remember to keep your shoulders down your back.

3 Feel your spine lifting off the mat, vertebra by vertebra. See how far you can extend yourself before you lose control of the movement.

4 Breathe in as you let your body slowly roll down to the mat, and breathe out as you come back up to the balanced position. Keep the movement slow and smooth as you repeat it 10 times.

the jack knife

NEW CHALLENGES

82

This is a strength manoeuvre that challenges you to lift the body up into a shoulder stand.

❗ CAUTION

Check that you have enough flexibility in the spine before you try this. By bending your knees during the movement you can reduce stress on the lower back.

emphasis	strength
visual cue	jack knife
repeat	10 times

1 Lie flat on the floor with your arms down by your side. Stretch your head away from you.

2 Breathe out and lift your legs slowly up to the ceiling. Keep your feet above your face as they stretch upwards. Try not to use your arms too much: use your centre as a powerhouse.

3 When you reach the highest point of your leg roll, slowly let your body come down to the floor again. It is not the stretch at the top of the movement that should be your goal but rather the journey getting there and coming back. The slower you do this movement, the more you will develop your strength.

hip twist

emphasis	strength
visual cue	toe
	hoops
repeat	10 times

1 From a seated position breathe out and contract your abs as you lift your legs to a balanced position. Your hands are by your side with your fingers pointing forward. Lift your head to the ceiling as you stretch your legs away from you.

2 Take a breath in preparation and keep your body in a fixed position. Then circle your legs away from you as you breathe out. Focus on your abs being the control point from which the impetus for the circling begins.

3 Complete the circle, holding the movement at the top and repeating it in the opposite direction. To lower the intensity you can lift the legs higher and bend your knees. You could also go back down onto your elbows. To really help you feel the effects of this exercise, then get a friend to hold your shoulders still. Do not allow them any movement as you perform the circles.

scissors

This is a strength movement that challenges you to stay balanced as you change legs.

❚ CAUTION

Don't let your leg drop towards you. It will help if you keep focused on the leg that is the furthest away from you. Let this leg lead the slow 'snipping' move.

emphasis	strength
visual cue	pair of scissors
repeat	10 times

1

2

3

1 Lie on the floor, arms by your sides. Breathe out as you lift your body into a shoulder-stand position using the movement of a jack knife (page 82). Place your hands behind your back for support.

2 Breathe out as open your legs an equal distance apart. Point your feet to the ceiling, stretching them as far as you can to lengthen the legs.

3 Breathe in as they close and change to the other side. Keep the movement consistent and slow as you find how wide you can take each 'snipping' move without your hips moving. Keep your hips pointing to the ceiling by using your abs to lift their weight off your elbows. Lengthen your neck and keep your shoulders pulled up, not crunched up.

scissors alternatives

The scissors can also be effective when it is performed closer to the floor. This will reduce the stress of gravity and make the movement easier to control. This alternative asks you to move your legs on a diagonal slope rather than on a vertical axis.

! CAUTION

Remember to keep your chin tucked in and begin the movement from your abs.

1 Lift up your legs until they form a diagonal slope. Slowly move your arms from your sides and point your fingers towards your toes.

2 Slowly move one leg down, keeping the other at the same height. Gently swap the legs around until you have completed the movement ten times.

the rocker

This move is designed to strengthen your back by curling it backwards.

! CAUTION

This movement extends and pulls the muscles in the lower back. If you feel uncomfortable stresses in your lower back it is better not to lift so high from the floor.

emphasis	strength
visual cue	rocking chair
repeat	10 times

1 Lie face down and lift your legs holding onto your feet. Pull your abs in so that a piece of paper could pass under your navel. Stretch your legs and push your ears foward.

2 Keeping the strength in your centre, lift your legs higher and breathe out. Take it to the point of tension that is most challenging.

3 Breathe in as you roll forward and breathe out as you roll back up. Keep the movement controlled, powering yourself from your centre.

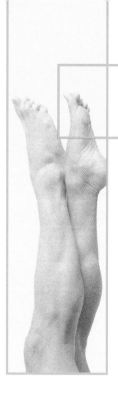

high intensity

These movements are the most challenging of all and will build strength and flexibility in equal measure. Only move on to these when you are confident that you are ready to do so. Remember all the vital elements of the Pilates technique as you attempt to perform them.

the boomerang

This movement is for mobility of the spine and uses your body weight and the weight of your legs.

! CAUTION

This is the hardest of the rolling series. With your legs fully extended, there will be strain on your back muscles so, as always, it is extremely important to remember to warm up. If you feel too much strain however, revert to the crab (page 74) or one of the other easier rolling series.

emphasis	mobility
visual cue	sling
	shot
repeat	10 times

1 Sit with your legs in front of you, your right leg crossed on top of your left. Reach your legs forward and pull in your abs. Keep your head upright and let your arms rest down by your sides. Move your shoulders so that they are open and rest down your back.

2 Lean your body forward and let your arms reach behind you. Fix the position of your body as you reach your point of tension.

3 Breathe in as you roll back up onto your shoulders. Keep your legs straight and use your arms as stabilisers. Breathe out as you come back up to the forward position. Control your legs as they gently touch the ground in front of you. Keep the movement smooth.

neck pull

emphasis	strength
visual cue	folding over
repeat	10 times

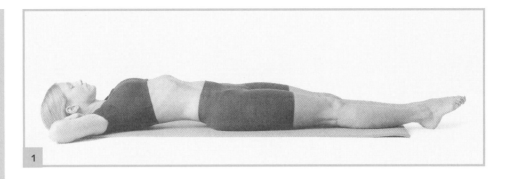

1 Lie on the floor with your arms behind your head and your fingers clasped. Stretch your legs out straight with your toes pointing away from you. Check your back is in neutral positon and you are pulling in on your centre.

2 Slowly roll forward and peel your back off the floor as you breathe out. Keep the movement very smooth and slow and if you feel any strain in your back then let your arms down. Pull in and up on your abs and bend your knees.

3 Stretch forward to the point of tension and then, without stopping, roll back down, laying your vertebrae onto the mat one by one. Try to be aware of each disc and to feel each vertebra imprint into your mat, imagining that the mat is made out of soft plasticine.

control balance

HIGH INTENSITY

88

This is the hardest of all of the movements as you have no stabilising arms to help you. It builds strength and challenges you to keep balance while moving your legs.

! CAUTION

Make sure you have enough flexibility to perform this under exercise with enough control.

emphasis	strength
visual cue	sprung coil
repeat	10 times

1 Lie on the floor with your back in a neutral position, your legs straight and your arms down by your sides.

2 Breathe out as you lift your legs slowly over your head until they touch the floor. Hold onto your ankles as you exhale.

3 Breathe in as you reach your right leg up to the ceiling, lengthening your body both up and behind you. Work from your powerhouse centre to maintain the balance.

4 Breathe out as you slowly change to the other leg without stopping, keeping the movement continuous as you pass through each point of the move.

5 After you have finished the series, breathe in and slowly lower the leg back down, breathing in so that both legs are above your head. Then roll back down to the mat, adopting the original position as you finally breathe out.

leg pull supine

This movement builds strength as you test your abs to keep your hips aloft while you move your legs.

❗ CAUTION

Keep your body weight off your shoulders by pulling your shoulder blades down your back and keeping your neck stretched long.

emphasis	strength
visual cue	Egyptian walk
repeat	10 times

1 Start in a sitting position with your legs straight in front of you. Place your hands on the floor, shoulder-width apart, with your fingers pointing towards your knees. Keep you head lifted up towards the ceiling. Pull your abs in and pull your shoulders down your back.

2 Breathe in as you raise your hips to the ceiling, making a straight line from your shoulders through your hips and ankles.

3 Breathe out as you raise your left leg to the ceiling keeping your hips in a fixed position. Focus on your centre of power to lift your legs. Breathe in as you lower one leg and change to the other. Repeat 10 times on each leg before lowering slowly. Keep the flow continuous as you change legs.

the corkscrew

emphasis	strength
visual cue	side
	twist
repeat	10 times

HIGH INTENSITY

90

1 Lie flat on the floor with your arms by your sides. Breathe out as you slowly raise your legs and torso up and over your head, letting your toes touch the floor. Slowly peel your back off the floor. Keep your arms down by your side to help you up off the floor and check your shoulders are pulled down your back. Breathe in when you reach the top point of the movement.

2 Breathe out and let your legs start drawing a semi-circle together. Start with a small circle to keep control and then try to find the point where you threaten to loose control. Feel the one side of your spine laying down on the floor as you complete the semi-circle.

3 As your tailbone touches the floor slowly breathe in and repeat the movement, lifting your legs up and over your head. This time, take the semi-circle to the other side. Work evenly on each side and remember the slower the movement, especially on the downward phase, the more strength you are building. Keep your actions continuous, flowing evenly.

rollover

1 Lie with your arms slightly out to the side and your feet pointing away from you. Slowly lift your legs from the ground and up over your head. Keep your toes pointed. Feel each vertebra lift up from the mat as you bring your legs further over the rest of your body.

2 Keep moving your legs until your feet gently touch the floor behind your head. Use your arms to keep control and maintain balance.

3 Continue the movement and bring your legs back up over your head. Try to keep the action continuous.

4 When your legs have come through the cycle and are back in position, open your legs until your toes reach beyond your hands. Do not attempt to open them too wide. Bring them together and begin the movement again.

tips to remember

Nearly all the Pilates movements require you to adopt some positions that may at first feel uncomfortable. Here, I've set out the best ways to think about how you should hold your body during the exercises. You need to assume the right positions in order to complete the movements correctly and to ensure that you do not inadvertently injure yourself.

abdominals

It is important to make sure you are breathing correctly when exercising your abdominal muscles. It is usual to find yourself breathing in when you pull in your abs and breathing out when your belly bulges. However, you need to do the opposite of this. Breathe out as you pull in your navel and tuck in your abdominal muscles.

When I talk about 'your centre' I am referring to the area that lies between your ribs and your hips. For many people, the abdominal muscles are the most neglected area of their bodies. Flabby bellies are testament to our neglect of this region. Simply tucking in the abs can often cause pain or short breath. Yet Joseph Pilates nicknamed the abdominal area 'the powerhouse' precisely because our entire body strength originates at our centre. The abdominals act as a second spine in that they support the back and help to keep us erect. The muscles comprise of various layers: the rectus abdominals, the internal and external obliques and the traversus abdominals. Some of the Pilates movements focus on the latter which are positioned around your midriff, much where a belt would lie on a pair of low-slung, hipster trousers. Through Pilates you will become more aware of your abs.

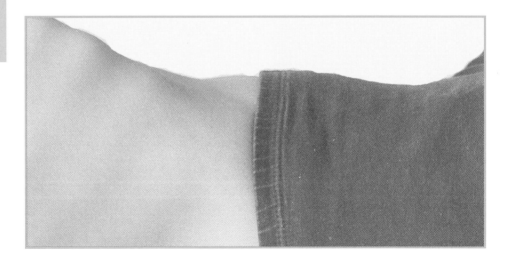

neck

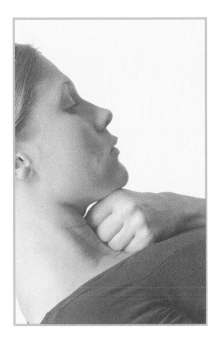

It is important for us to build the neck strength as the neck supports the weight of the head. On average one head weighs between 14 and 18 lbs. Many Pilates exercises expect us to be able to carry this weight, but like any strengthening process, it can take time. If you feel at any point that there is too much stress on your neck, then put your hands behind your head. It is very important that your head is in alignment with the rest of your body when you perform the movements. I have found the easiest way to check this is to put my fist between my chin and chest so that my head rests just on top of it. Another good check is to imagine that you are holding an orange under your chin. This stops you jutting your chin forward and straining your neck muscles or jamming your chin onto your chest. Use these methods to check that you are performing the movements correctly. If you have a stiff neck in the morning after doing these movements then you have pushed your self a little too much. The next time you practise, put your arms back to support your head much sooner.

shoulders

In all of the movements, your shoulder muscles should be pulled well down your back. When we try to use our shoulders in strength movements, it is normal to find that they have a tendancy to rise up our backs and hunch up around the neck. Stand up straight and feel the position in which ideally they should remain. I like to think of them as two plates that I need to slide down my back. When you put your shoulders in position down your back, your chest will automatically push forward and out and you will find that your whole appearance and look changes. Try to maintain this shoulder position when you are sitting and standing. At the beginning you will have to think constantly about adjusting your shoulders but, with time, you will find you can adopt this pose more easily and more naturally.

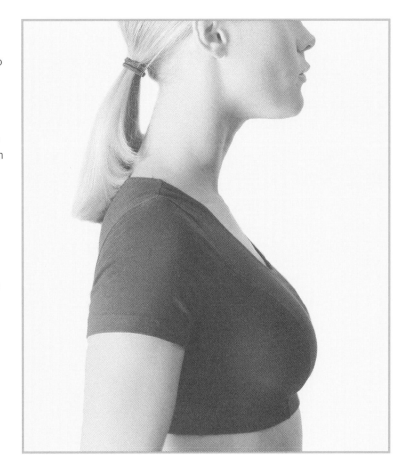

glossary

Abdominal muscles (abs): the muscles layered across the midriff that lie across each other at various angles. There are four types: the rectus abdominals, internal obliques, external obliques and transversus abdominals.

Aerobic exercise: any sustained activity that works the heart and lungs, increasing the amount of oxygen in the blood.

Alignment: arrangement in a straight line.

Cardiovascular: relating to the heart or the blood vessels.

Centering movements: the Pilates exercises that work the centre of the body, abdominals and back.

Core exercises: the Pilates movements that concentrate on strengthening the abdominal and back muscles.

Crunching: sit-ups where the abdominals are not engaged so much as squeezed together, shortening the space between the hips and ribcage.

Contrology: the name given by Joseph Pilates to his exercise method which he defined as "the science and art of coordinated body–mind–spirit development through natural movements under strict control of the will."

C-shape: the shape of the spine when the body is slumped over and bent due to bad posture.

Elongation: lengthening of the muscle. Leaner muscles develop from stretching the muscle rather than bulking it up.

Hidden stress: when muscle groups compensate for an injury or difficulty by using larger muscles to protect weaker ones.

Hunching: result of neck and shoulder tension within the trapezius muscles. Muscles here can tense up in a defensive automatic reaction.

Hyperextention: extending further than 180 degrees. This occurs when the muscles tense up and the elbows or knees lock, resulting in a reverse bending.

Imprinting: gently pushing each vertebra into the mat, as though it were leaving an indentation.

Lumbar curve: the bend of the spine at the small of the back.

Overloading: point where the effort required by a muscle to withstand an applied weight is too great. The tissue may tear or rupture as a result.

Powerhouse: The name that Joseph Pilates gave to the abdominal area, found between our ribcage and

hips. Pilates exercises work this area in order to create a stronger, more balanced lower back.

Prone: lying face downwards.

Resistance: an opposing force that pulls in the opposite direction to the one created by your muscle.

Rolling: exercises where the spine rolls over the mat, one vertebra at a time.

Soft knees: holding the knees relaxed and slightly bent, rather than locked.

Supine: lying down on the back.

Tendon: elastic linking tissue that connects bone to muscle.

Tripod position: where the feet support the body weight by distributing it evenly over three points: the ball of the foot, the middle of the heel and the outside edge of the foot, near the little toe.

Vertebra: one of the bony segments that make up the spinal column.

Visualisation: use of mental imagery to aid the accomplishment of physical tasks – an important element of the Pilates technique that helps the mind more effectively control the body.

index

A

abdominal muscles 36, 92
  breathing 34
    roll up 23, 24, 25, 60-1
advanced movements 25, 86-91
Alexander technique 8
arms
  double arm circles 53
  one arm circles 52
  toy soldier 53

B

Bacall, Lauren 8
back
  boomerang 25, 86
  corkscrew 25, 90
  crab 24, 25, 74
  curves 28, 73
  neutral spine 73
  pain 28
  posture 12
  rocker 24, 25, 85
  rocker with open legs 24, 25, 76
  rollover 91
  round back 51
  the saw 23, 24, 25, 68
  the seal 23, 24, 25, 29, 66
  shoulder bridge 24, 25, 77
  shoulder bridge preparation 23, 24, 25, 69
  spine stretch 23, 24, 25, 71
  spine twist 23, 24, 25, 29, 72-3
balance 36
  control balance 25, 88
  side bend 24, 25, 78-9
  side kick 23, 24, 25, 70
Balanchine, George 16-18
beds 29
body, listening to 61
Body Control Studios 6
boomerang 25, 86
breathing 23, 34

C

cars, driving posture 29
Cash, Pat 8
centering 36
chest stretch 51
Cirque de Soleil 40
concentration 32
control 38
control balance 25, 88
corkscrew 25, 90
crab 24, 25, 74

D

diaphragm, breathing 34
double arm circles 53
double leg stretch 24, 25, 29, 75
driving posture 29

F

feet, balance 36
Feldenkrais 8
Fletcher, Ron 18-19
Foster, Jodie 8
functional exercises 12

G

goals 20
Graham, Martha 18
Grant, Kathy 19
Greece, Ancient 19

H

hip twist 24, 25, 83
history of Pilates 16-19
home, posture in 28
Houston Ballet 6
the hundred 23, 24, 25, 29, 64-5

I

isolation 44

J

jack knife 24, 25, 82
Japan 12
Joseph Pilates 8, 14, 16

K

Kryzanowska, Romana 18

L

legs
  boomerang 86
  control balance 88
  corkscrew 90
  double leg stretch 24, 25, 29, 75
  hip twist 24, 25, 83
  leg pull prone 23, 24, 25, 58-9
  leg pull supine 25, 89
  one leg circle 23, 24, 25, 63
  one leg stretch 23, 24, 25, 67
  rocker with open legs 24, 25, 76
  rollover 91
  scissors 24, 25, 84-5
  side kick 23, 24, 25, 70
  side-kick kneeling 24, 25, 80
  teaser 81
Leonardo da Vinci 40
listening to your body 61
London School of Contemporary Dance 6
lying posture 29

M

Madonna 8, 20
mattresses 29
mind/body techniques 8
movement 42
muscles
  stretching 10, 23
  synergy 44

N

neck 93
  neck pull 25, 87
neutral spine 73
New York City Ballet 18
Nimura, Yeichi 19

O

office workers, posture 28
one arm circles 52
one leg circle 23, 24, 25, 63
one leg stretch 23, 24, 25, 67
oxygen, breathing 23

P

pain, preventing 26-9
Peck, Gregory 8
Pilates, Clara 16, 18, 19
Pilates, Joseph 8, 14, 16-19,
  23, 28
Pilates Studio, New York 18
posture 12, 28
precision 40
programmes 22-5
push-up 23, 24, 25, 54-5

R

rest 61
rocker 24, 25, 85
rocker with open legs 24, 25, 76

roll back 23, 24, 25, 62
roll-up 23, 24, 25, 60-1
rolling 29
rollover 25, 91
round back 51
routines 46

S

San Miguel, Lolita 19
the saw 23, 24, 25, 68
scissors 24, 25, 84-5
the seal 23, 24, 25, 29, 66
Seed, Bob 18
shoulder bridge 24, 25, 69, 77
shoulder bridge preparation 23,
  24, 25, 69
shoulder stand
  jack knife 82
  scissors 84-5
shoulders 93
side bend 24, 25, 78-9
side kick 23, 24, 25, 70
side kick kneeling 24, 25, 80
sit-ups 36
sitting posture 28-9
sleep 61
Sleep, Wayne 8
slouching 28
sofas 28-9
spine, see back

stress 32
supine position 73
swimming 23, 24, 25, 29,
  56-7
swinging 50
symmetry 12

T

tai chi 42
teaser 24, 25, 81
television, and posture 28-9
torso
  abdominal muscles 36, 92
  hip twist 24, 25, 83
  the hundred 23, 24, 25,
    29, 64-5
  neck pull 25, 87
toy soldier 53
Trier, Carola 18, 19

V

Valsalvic breathing 34

W

warm-ups 50-3
weaknesses, identifying 20
weight loss 20, 44

Y

yoga 8

INDEX/ACKNOWLEDGEMENTS

acknowledgements

I would like to thank my mother and family for being so supportive of me, a boy from Scunthorpe, a Northern steelworks town, who wanted to go to dance school. (Thanks John Travolta for making it OK for men to dance.) I must also sincerely thank my mentor and teacher Alan Herdman, who first inspired me to pursue Pilates as a career, and the many other Pilates teachers who have shared their knowledge with me. Thanks to my friend David, who told me I wasn't crazy when I wanted to open my own studio at Pineapple when no-one had ever heard of Pilates. To my friends at Houston Ballet who made me feel like the city was my second home. To Malcolm, for all his support and encouragement through this incredible last year. To all at Mitchell Beazley publishers, especially Rachael, Emma, Mary, Frances and Kenny for their sweet demeanors and cool heads as deadlines approached. And finally, I thank all those who have attended my classes all over the world over the years. It's been great!

Photographic credits, GOS = Getty One Stone: 10, 11 GOS/Lori Adamski Peek; 14,15 GOS/Adri Berger; 16, 17 Balanced Body; 18 GOS/David Ash; 20, 21; Retna Pictures Ltd; 26, 27 GOS/K Dan-Bergman; 49 GOS/David Ash
All other photographs by Ruth Jenkenson

BUILDING A BETTER WORLD

100 stories of co-operation

BY KATE ASKEW

AUTHOR'S NOTE

While collecting stories for this book, the most revealing moment occurred during a conversation with a development worker in Africa. The worker noted that the co-operatives with which the NGO was working had not only survived once the NGO had concluded its program – they had flourished. "Do you know how often that happens?" I was asked. "Never." The word that best describes the work co-operatives do is 'powerful'.

The power of co-operatives to transform businesses, industries and, particularly, individuals, can be jaw-dropping. This is as true of small co-operatives in developing countries as it is of major businesses in some of the world's most significant economies.

It would be remiss not to mention the extreme difficulties and ordeals endured by some co-operative members featured in this book – fighting for two decades to gain access to ancestral land; rebuilding a community via a co-operative after 45 people were gunned down in a church; co-operatives piecing together a country's economy after it has been destroyed by war – these are stories that resonate through lifetimes.

They demonstrate a way forward for the rest of us.

Kate Askew, April 2012

EDITOR'S NOTE

Some co-operatives for historical or political reasons call themselves unions or associations.

BUILDING A
BETTER WORLD

100 stories of co-operation

BY KATE ASKEW

CONTENTS

AUTHOR'S NOTE   2

ROLL OF HONOUR   6

ACKNOWLEDGEMENTS   8

INTRODUCTION   10

FOREWORD   11

Québec City, Canada   12
Kenya   16

CHAPTER 1:
RECOVERING FROM
CRISIS AND CONFLICT   18

Acteal, Mexico   20
Tavush, Armenia   21
Kitgum, Uganda   22
Phnom Penh, Cambodia   23
Port-au-Prince, Haiti   24
Bucharest, Romania   25
Congo   26
Niassa, Mozambique   27
Lesotho   28
Deir Kanoun Ras El Eins, Lebanon   29

CHAPTER 2:
HEALING ABUSE AND
FEEDING THE HUNGRY   30

Kathmandu, Nepal   32
Lake Atitlán, Guatemala   33
India   34
Zambia   35
Gujarat, India   36
Abidjan, Ivory Coast   38
Finland   39

CHAPTER 3:
STARTING NEW LIVES   40

Sous Valley, Morocco   42
Sharjah, United Arab Emirates   43
Benin   44
Washington State, USA   45
Cumbria, United Kingdom   46
Eastern Dzongkhags, Bhutan   47
Pennsylvania, USA   48
Ghana, Liberia, Kenya, Uganda   50
Terrace, Canada   51
Malta   52
USA; Canada   53
Arctic, Canada   54

CHAPTER 4:
EMPOWERING WORKERS   56

Chilavert, Argentina   58
Luzon, Philippines   59
Sumilao, Philippines   60
Beijing, China   61
Córdoba, Argentina   62
Tver, Russia   63
Kumasi, Ghana   64
Villa Domínico, Argentina   66
Ulaanbaatar and Govi-Altai, Mongolia 67
Jargalant Soum, Mongolia   68
Christchurch, New Zealand   69

CHAPTER 5: SUPPORTING CO-OPERATIVES	70
United States	72
Scotland	74
Poland	76
Washington, USA	78
Canada	79
Malaysia	80
Canada	82
Worldwide	84
Iran	85

CHAPTER 6: BATTLING BIG BUSINESS	86
Scotland; England	88
Glasgow, Scotland	89
Kalamazoo, USA	90
Berlin, Germany	91
Leicester, England	92
Sweden; Norway	93
Australia; New Zealand	94

CHAPTER 7: HAVING A POSITIVE INFLUENCE	96
France; Québec, Ontario, Canada	98
Horsens, Denmark	99
Calgary, Canada	100
Chapecó, Brazil	102
Slovakia	103
United Kingdom	104
Seoul, South Korea	106
Canada	108
British Columbia, Canada	110
Santo André, Brazil	112
Malaysia	113
Trentino, Italy	114
Bogotá, Colombia	115
Singapore	116
Iran	118
Lisbon, Portugal	119
India	120
Brussels, Belgium	122
Githunguri, Kenya	124
Western Australia; Southeast Asia	125
Toronto, Canada	128

CHAPTER 8: INSPIRING CHANGE	130
Mondragón, Spain	132
Germany	133
Western Canada	134
Japan	138
Nadi, Fiji	139
Laguna, Philippines	140
Bologna, Italy	141
Nova Petrópolis, Brazil	142
Asunción, Paraguay	143
Arnhem Land, Australia	144

CHAPTER 9: DELIVERING BENEFITS	146
Japan	148
San José, Costa Rica	149
Bangladesh	150
Pune, India	151
Stockholm, Sweden	152
Karachi, Pakistan	154
Montevideo, Uruguay	155
Beit She'an Valley, Israel	156
Azezo, Ethiopia	157
San Salvador, El Salvador	158

ROLL OF HONOUR

THIS BOOK HAS BEEN MADE POSSIBLE BY THE GENEROUS SUPPORT
OF THE FOLLOWING CO-OPERATIVES AND ORGANISATIONS

PLATINUM PARTNERS

Federated Co-operatives
    Limited (FCL), Canada
Desjardins, Canada

SILVER PARTNERS

Angkasa, Malaysia
Arctic Co-operatives
    Limited (ACL), Canada
The Big Carrot, Canada
Calgary Co-op, Canada
The Co-operative Group,
    United Kingdom
Co-operative Insurance
    Company (CIC), Kenya
The Co-operators, Canada
Scottish Agricultural Organisation
    Society (SAOS), Scotland
Indian Farmers Fertiliser Cooperative
    Ltd (IFFCO), India
HSB Housing Co-operatives, Sweden
National Agricultural Co-operative
    Federation (NACF), Korea
National Auditing Union of Workers'
    Co-operatives (NAUWC), Poland
National Cooperative Grocers
    Association (NCGA), United States
NTUC FairPrice Co-operative
    Limited, Singapore
On Co-op, Canada
Saint Mary's University, Canada
University of Saskatchewan, Canada
Université de Sherbrooke, Canada
Vancity, Canada

BRONZE PARTNERS

Canadian Co-operative
    Association, Canada
Central Union of Rural and Agricultural
    Cooperatives (Curaci), Iran
Conseil canadien de la coopération
    et de la mutualité, Canada
Conseil québécois de la coopération
    et de la mutualité, Canada
Iran Chamber of Commerce (ICC), Iran

Shift Urban Cargo Delivery hauls cargo throughout downtown Vancouver using pedal-driven, heavy-duty cargo trikes, giving exceptional service while emitting zero greenhouse gases. Vancity financed a line of credit to help Shift meet its capital needs, and Vancity Community Foundation supplied a grant through the Social Enterprise Portfolio Program.

ACKNOWLEDGEMENTS

People from all corners of the world threw themselves into this book in the very spirit of co-operation. Without the years of research conducted by European Research Institute on Cooperative and Social Enterprises (Euricse) fellow Marcelo Vieta, which he so generously shared, the vital stories of co-operative activism in Argentina would never have found their way into these pages. Equally, Sally Hartley from the Co-operative College was extremely generous with her research conducted in Lesotho. Then there were people like Raul 'Soc' Socrates who went to great lengths to provide the powerful stories of agrarian co-operative reform in the Philippines. I was so pleased to be able to include the story of the Benin mothers' co-operatives, with the help of Shirley Burchfield and Al Miller from World Education. For her explanations of Fairtrade and the global coffee industry, including the story of Maya Vinic, I want to thank Monika Firl of Coop Coffees.

Without the help of the excellent communications staff at the UN Food and Agriculture Organisation (FAO) in Rome, including Maarten Roest, Carina Hirsch and Denis Herbel, the book would be without several stories. Thanks to Heiko Bammann on the ground in the Solomon Islands. In India, Poonam Shroff became my eyes and ears at the extraordinary SEWA organisation. On the African continent no-one was as generous with their time as Anna Tibblin at the Swedish Co-operative Centre, along with Henrik Brundin and the centre's many staff including Diamantino Nhampossa and Celia Enosse. Thanks to Jim Ford at NRECA for his insights into how co-operative development programs really work on the ground. And many thanks to Karma Yanka for excellent background on Bhutan co-operatives.

Vanessa Smith was not only a connecting force with the Latin American co-operative insurance sector, but also a translator and guide. John Gully and his team at ICMIF went to great lengths to assist in sourcing insurance stories. At OCB in Brazil, Fabiola da Silva, Nader Motta, Tania Regina Zanella and Joana Laura Marinho Nogueira were a delight to work with. The ACI Americas' Manuel Mariño and Christina DeCastro at ICA Expo assisted greatly. Euricse's Ilana Bodini of www.stories.coop helped out when most needed and, indeed, without Euricse's desire to tell stories this project would not have begun. Oxfam's help was indispensable.

In the closing stages of writing this book I was so very happy to meet Altantuya in Mongolia, who helped with several stories from a country that was instrumental in ensuring that the co-operative movement had this UN year to celebrate. At the opening stages it was a pleasure to work with Shimelles Tenaw, who gave me a helpful overview of both the Finnish co-operative sector and co-operative traditions in Ethiopia.

Without Phil Jones's dogged belief in this project and his work ethic this book would undoubtedly never have eventuated. Monica Lawrie's passion for this kind of book shines through in her beautiful design work and layout, a correct tribute to the many individuals behind the splendid co-operatives in this book. Fastidious editing by Mark Derby and Melina Morrison's help as a sounding board also ensured this book became a storytelling victory.

Last but not least, I want to acknowledge the terrific support and faith of the financial partners in this publication. It is the first book of its kind in the sector, and without these forward-looking individuals the co-operative movement would be without an official record of its vibrant and inspiring elements in this UN International Year. Unfortunately, I don't have enough space to thank everyone personally, but Richard Lacasse from Desjardins and Vic Huard from Federated Cooperatives were not only delightful to work with, but also exceptional practitioners. Michael Mugo from CIC in Kenya and Karolina Rozjek at NAUWC in Poland were enormously efficient and Babak Khoshnevisan and Yadi in Iran also. The Canadian co-operative sector generally is one of the most organised and professional – many thanks to everyone involved in making this project a success.

Leverandørselskabet Danish Crown Amba, Denmark.

INTRODUCTION

DAME PAULINE GREEN
PRESIDENT, INTERNATIONAL CO-OPERATIVE ALLIANCE
GENEVA, SWITZERLAND

This book is a tribute to some of the most inspirational co-operative enterprises around the world.

Many of the stories featured demonstrate the spirit of people at grassroots level as they seek to create a new and better future, often out of adversity. It also shines a light on the value of the co-operative model of business itself which, through its global set of principles and values, gives ordinary folk the ability to take themselves out of poverty with dignity. It shows the power of the co-operative values and principles that have helped to embed civil society around the world for more than 170 years by creating sustainable community owned and controlled enterprises.

The book is sponsored by some of the world's largest and most successful co-operatives. They have put their name to the book in celebration of the great gift that the worldwide co-operative movement was given by the United Nations when they declared 2012 the International Year of Co-operatives, but also to pool their combined endeavours to ensure that these truly pioneering stories receive the daylight they so deserve.

Worldwide, co-operatives are united in a huge and growing network of local, autonomous, sovereign businesses, in a multitude of different sectors of the economy, that have developed according to local needs, local culture and member demands. Equally at home in any political, religious or cultural environment, our primary constitutional objective is to give our member owners a good deal, not simply to maximise profits.

Co-operatives are about human need and not human greed.

As 2012 draws to a close, the movement is in confident mood and ready for the future. Owned by nearly one billion people across the globe, employing more than 100 million people worldwide, and representing micro businesses through to global institutions, co-operatives know that they can do much more to support individuals, families and communities in the coming decades.

Dame Pauline Green
President
International Co-operative Alliance

FOREWORD

JOSÉ GRAZIANO DA SILVA
DIRECTOR-GENERAL
FOOD AND AGRICULTURE ORGANISATION OF THE UNITED NATIONS

Co-operatives represent a resourceful and diverse enterprise model that has great resilience to financial, economic and environmental shocks. Agricultural co-operatives, in particular, have a significant impact on employment, wealth generation, poverty reduction and food security.

Co-operatives allow small producers to act collectively and network more effectively, thus improving their livelihoods and overall wellbeing. They provide a variety of services ranging from access to markets, to access and management of natural resources and a voice in decision-making. As such, they often have a direct influence on food security.

In Egypt, four million farmers earn their income thanks to membership in agricultural and food co-operatives. In Brazil, agricultural co-operatives have more than one million members and generate 37 percent of the agricultural GDP. Worldwide, co-operatives employ 100 million people.

Agricultural and food co-operatives, as member-owned enterprises, contribute to socio-economic development and enable the self-empowerment of the poor and other marginalised groups in rural areas. They have also proven to be a vehicle for social inclusion, in particular by encouraging the involvement of youth and promoting gender equality.

FAO has renewed its commitment to support agricultural and food co-operatives and other small-scale producer organisations by engaging in partnerships and diverse types of collaboration. FAO encourages governments to establish favourable policies and legal frameworks that support the development and strengthening of agricultural co-operatives. The International Year of Co-operatives represents a unique opportunity to do so.

Strong agricultural co-operatives are key to feeding the world, as this year's World Food Day theme clearly states.

José Graziano da Silva
Director-General
Food and Agriculture Organisation of the United Nations

QUÉBEC CITY, CANADA
INTERNATIONAL SUMMIT OF COOPERATIVES, OCTOBER 2012

The International Summit of Cooperatives taking place on 8–11 October 2012 will provide a strategic meeting place for managers of the entire spectrum of co-operative and mutual enterprises committed to finding solutions to the development and performance challenges they all share.

In its inaugural year in Québec City, Canada, the summit will offer a program based on the release of nine groundbreaking multi-sector studies, and will welcome more than 130 world-renowned speakers, including Nobel Prize recipients and leaders from both the business and academic worlds.

These leaders will identify and provide solutions to help co-operatives tackle today's and tomorrow's business issues and promote the co-operative model on a global basis.

By bringing together these individuals, this first summit will be the genesis of a worldwide co-operative network which, over time, will create a powerful sphere of influence in both economic and political arenas.

This summit and future summits will ensure that co-operatives and mutuals take their rightful place on the world stage.

The 2012 International Summit of Cooperatives will be the 'Davos' of the co-operative movement.

QUÉBEC, CANADA
DESJARDINS GROUP

Desjardins Group CEO Monique Leroux outlines her plans for the future, while keeping one eye on the past.

Monique F. Leroux rests in an armchair in front of the oil portraits of Alphonse and Dorimène Desjardins in Desjardins Group's headquarters in Lévis, Québec.

Leroux's ease is plain. Perhaps it has something to do with the connection she feels between these co-founders' vision for what is now Canada's sixth largest financial institution, and what she is working towards today.

Since her election in 2008 as Desjardins' Chair of the Board, President and CEO, Leroux has introduced changes to the Group's governance practices, which has broadened the role of its 5,400 local elected officers.

Alphonse Desjardins arrived at his made-in-Canada model for a co-operative financial enterprise in 1900 after consulting fellow co-operators Henry Wolff from England, Luigi Luzzatti from Italy, and Charles Rayneri and Louis Durand from France.

Likewise, Leroux is putting in place her own co-operative relationships with Crédit Mutuel of France, and each now has a liaison office in the other's country. "It doesn't cost a lot, but it is precious. To have a foot in Europe is to be better in touch with key people," says Leroux. She has also put in place a research sharing agreement with ESN North America, a broking house majority-owned by an arm of Crédit Mutuel.

In these uncertain financial times, Leroux, the former senior Vice-President of a major Canadian Bank, and prior to that a managing partner at Ernst & Young, holds the view that a balanced economic environment is achieved through a three-part model – private, public and co-operative. "We can't expect the economy alone to provide a balanced economic model - we have to regulate down."

All indications show that it is time to embrace that three-part model, says Leroux. Asked about the Occupy movement and its rage against capitalism, she says the protesters highlighted a disconnection between the general public and the financial market elite. "There are some challenges before us and we must take those phenomena into account," she says. Finance, in her well-regarded opinion, exists to support the "real economy" and not solely derivatives markets.

But, as Leroux points out, it's not the first time Desjardins has operated in a difficult environment. When Alphonse and Dorimène founded the first Desjardins *caisse* (credit union) in Lévis in December 1900, the economy was also in the doldrums.

Most of the population had no access to loans due to the poor outlook for business profit. Those who could raise money did so on usurious terms. Desjardins' model ensured that everyone – from the less well-to-do farmer to the better-off merchant – had access to financial services.

The model Alphonse derived from Europe put people, and therefore the needs of society, first. It offered self-empowerment and an expectation that its actions would serve the common good. Money working for people, not the other way around.

Leroux remains fond of Alphonse's sage words from that time:

More than ever before people are struggling on the economic battlefield. Now that communications are easier and more rapid, the market has become a world market, and the definitive victory will go to the country that has succeeded in marshalling all its energies and all the vital forces of its citizens, that has succeeded best in supporting their initiatives and that as a consequence has adopted the most productive plan with the least effort.

With its 5.6 million members and close to CAD 200 billion dollars in assets, Desjardins can claim its own definitive victory on many levels. In 2012, it was ranked 18th in *Global Finance*'s World's 50 Safest Banks and won the first position among "Best 50 Corporate Citizens in Canada" published by *Corporate Knights* magazine. In the same year it was among the *Financial Post*'s Ten Best Companies to Work For in Canada. In 2010, Waterstone Human Capital ranked it one of Canada's 10 Most Admired Corporate Cultures and United Kingdom-based *The Banker* selected it as Canada's Bank of the Year.

With a swag of personal awards ranging from *Finance et Investissement*'s Québec Financial Person of the Year for 2012, to the Woodrow Wilson Award for her contribution to Canadian society, and being named one of 25 Transformational Canadians by *Globe & Mail*, CTV and *La Presse*, Monique Leroux can feel equally confident of her direction. Now her attention is on future victories – as always, with one eye on past lessons.

Desjardins

Cooperating in building the future

KENYA
CO-OPERATIVE INSURANCE COMPANY (CIC)

"We keep our word" is the motto of the CIC (Co-operative Insurance Company) Insurance Group, a leading provider of insurance and related financial services in Kenya, and a leading co-operative insurer in Africa. The company is competing strongly with both commercial insurers and multinational firms in Kenya. It commands a sizeable market share in the Kenyan insurance industry, holding second place out of 46 companies in 2011. CIC is the market leader in providing insurance services to the co-operative and low-income market segments in the country. It has been a pioneer in micro-insurance both locally and internationally, and its drive to increase insurance penetration has earned it international recognition.

CIC is also the preferred underwriter of the co-operative movement in Kenya, whose members act both as shareholders and clients of the company. Over the last 10 years, CIC has transformed into one of the most successful local companies. In 2011, its gross premium was USD 79 million, a growth rate of 48 percent compared to USD 54 million in 2010. Profit before tax grew by an impressive 30 percent to USD 9.2 million from USD 7.1 million. The company's 48 percent growth in assets, from USD 88.2 million to USD 130.5 million, was well above the industry average rate.

CIC recognises the critical role played by employees in realising its strategic objectives. The company has placed human capital development at centre stage, and has won several awards for its application of the co-operative philosophy in developing people.

The transformation of CIC can largely be attributed to its entrepreneurial nature and inventive spirit. Its business philosophy is built on the four pillars of – service of highest quality, friendliest of relationships, fairest prices and fastest speed. For example, CIC departed from the norm following the post-election violence that engulfed Kenya in 2007/8, when many small and medium businesses were burnt down or vandalised. The company came out very strongly in support of compensation for the victims, and paid claims worth USD 1.2 million.

CIC is also very strong in the micro-insurance sector in Kenya and has played a pioneering role. One of the landmark marketing programs of the CIC Insurance Group, the M-Bima initiative, has also received global recognition, in particular from the International Labour Organisation (ILO) Microinsurance Innovation Facility in Geneva. With backing from the ILO, various market research activities are taking place, including focus group discussions with sample groups of M-BIMA clients. This feedback is helping CIC develop its future marketing plan, which includes branding, communication and distribution.

A recent survey of Kenya's micro-insurance landscape identified the main areas as health protection, life cover (and in particular cover for funeral costs) and the risks associated with agricultural production. Generally, the cost of health in Kenya is relatively high, and delivering health insurance to the low-income market poses unique challenges. The difficulty of claims management and high administration expenses have made it increasingly difficult to design appropriate health micro-insurance cover.

Despite this, CIC is piloting a new and improved health micro-insurance cover called Afya Imara (Swahili for 'good health'). The product offers both inpatient and outpatient cover as an affordable family package. The main challenge in health insurance is normally outpatient cover, as this has high levels of uptake and can potentially lead to a very high claims ratio. In the product design stage, CIC negotiated with mission and low-cost hospitals around the country to offer services to Afya Imara clients at a subsidised rate. As a result, CIC has been able to provide highly discounted health insurance. To reduce administration expenses, CIC has approached co-operative societies and micro-finance institutions to extend this cover to their members. These institutions are also offering insurance premium financing to ease the burden of payment.

CIC INSURANCE GROUP LTD
We keep our word

CHAPTER 1

*Recovering from crisis
and conflict*

ACTEAL, MEXICO

Eight-month-old Juana Vasquez Luna was the youngest victim to be gunned down in a Roman Catholic church three days before Christmas in 1997. While fasting and at prayer, the members of the civil movement La Sociedad Civil Las Abejas ('the Bees') were attacked by about 90 members of the paramilitary groups Paz e Justicia (Peace and Justice) and Mascara Roja (Red Mask). Of the 45 indigenous people killed, 21 were women, 15 children and nine men, mostly elders. Four of the women were pregnant.

The 12-hour killing spree in the small highland Mexican town of Acteal, in the state of Chiapas, was a reaction to the Bees' movement's efforts to gain autonomous development. Two years later this civil movement gave rise to the producers' union Maya Vinic, a coffee-producing co-operative comprising more than 500 families, which recognises traditional, co-operative ways of organising their communities.

Coffee farming began in this region in the lowland country in the 1900s. Indigenous highlanders were recruited to work on the plantations during coffee harvesting periods, and these lowly paid workers took seeds back to the highlands, where they began to produce their own coffee beans.

Maya Vinic's members are now drawn from 38 different highland communities in the Chiapas municipalities of Chenalhó, Pantelhó and Chalchihuitán. They each farm about an acre and produce on average 400 kilos of coffee beans from each plot. A general assembly is responsible for overall organisation, and an assembly of community delegates works closely with the producers' board of directors.

The coffee the Maya Vinic members produce is registered under the Fairtrade brand, yet the people of Acteal believe there was nothing fair about the 1997 massacre, which orphaned 54 children. Those responsible for this act of genocide have still not been brought to justice. Yet the co-operative borne of this bloodshed thrives. It has given its members economic autonomy even when political power was out of reach.

TAVUSH, ARMENIA

Armenia's mountainous expanses are home to many historical treasures, including the first church in the world to be built by a state. The country also has a unique alphabet. Yet, for all its rich cultural history, this eastern European nation, with its high-altitude climate of long, cold and snowy winters and dry, hot summers, is a testing place to live.

Formerly part of the Soviet Union, this landlocked part of the south Caucasus declared its independence in 1990. It was the first non-Baltic nation in the Soviet Union to do so, but the road to economic independence has not been smooth. Armenia's borders with Turkey to its west and Azerbaijan to its east are closed.

Turkey does not recognise the Armenian genocide of 1915, and fighting continues over the disputed border with Azerbaijan. The border closures have been problematic for the Armenian economy, as all trade in and out of the country has been halted.

In 1994, Oxfam joined the growing list of non-governmental organisations (NGOs) and organisations, including the World Bank, working to assist Armenia. Oxfam has established co-operatives in 10 poor, rural communities to help more than 340 farmer households with more than 1,500 direct beneficiaries.

One of the poorest regions in the northeast of the country, Tavush province is home to the Aknaghbur Agricultural Consumer Co-operative. Among its 37 small farm-holders is 80-year-old Shaghik Mkhitaryan. She, like many other producers, cultivates traditional Armenian crops such as figs, persimmons, cornelian cherries and mulberries.

Climate change has had a damaging impact on the region's agriculture, bringing increased hailstorms, early and late spring frosts, and heavy rainfall. As a result, Shaghik has begun cultivating non-traditional crops, which cope better with the harsher climate – crops like cherry tomatoes, chillies and broccoli.

Armenians like Shaghik are working together to bring sustainability to the troubled nation's rural communities and economies.

KITGUM, UGANDA

*He who has never had a sorrow
cannot speak words of comfort.*

– UGANDAN PROVERB

Travel agents may refer to Uganda as the Pearl of Africa, but people
living in the landlocked east African country have had to endure
21 years of civil war.

This is particularly apparent in the country's north where almost
two million people were displaced by the atrocities of dictator Idi
Amin. Amin was succeeded by a series of war-installed presidents
who perpetuated his behaviour, most notably Joseph Kony and his
Lord's Resistance Army.

A return to life without war is the best that Ugandan people can
expect. Thousands have nowhere to go. They remain in mud huts
in the internally displaced persons' camps because water is easier
to come by there.

Most of the displaced populations in this part of the country
have no way of returning to their homelands. They are busy enough
trying to reintegrate young men who had been kidnapped to work
as soldiers, and young girls who were kidnapped and made into
sex slaves.

Despite this situation, the Kitgum Savings and Credit
Co-operative has deliberately set up operations in this devastated
northern part of the country. It is helping to fund start-up businesses,
many of them begun by women using inventive means to make
handicrafts, or market gardens to produce vegetables. Some tend
goats and chickens.

The women have set up collectives that allow loan funding to be
raised from the credit co-operative. In all, about 18,000 people in this
part of Uganda are being helped with these micro-loans.

*This story was made possible with the help of Kimberley Ney,
who travelled to Uganda with the Canadian Co-operative Association.*

PHNOM PENH, CAMBODIA

The members of the Watthan Artisans Cooperative like to say that they focus on their abilities, not their disabilities.

In the late 1970s, Pol Pot and the Communist Khmer Rouge regime left Cambodia's economy teetering. Pol Pot's infamous 'killing fields' were mass graves. The number of Cambodians who died there, together with those who succumbed to starvation and disease, is estimated at between 1.7 and 2.5 million, from a total population of eight million.

The Watthan Artisans' Cooperative brings together some of those people who endured the after-effects of the Pol Pot regime. It was formed in 2004 to provide work for people bearing injuries from landmines and bombs, suffering from deafness, psychological scars or the aftermath of polio. They were supported by an NGO, which trained them to work with cotton, locally produced silk, reclaimed hardwood and recycled materials.

As one of the co-operative's members, Try Suphereac, explained, "The NGO was closed and the co-operative took its place. It gives work and ownership to trained and talented craftsmen who might otherwise find it difficult to work."

These men and women are paid on the basis of their abilities, not their disabilities.

PORT-AU-PRINCE, HAITI

The Haitian capital of Port-au-Prince still lies in ruins after the devastating earthquake of January 2010. Haiti has the largest population of any Caribbean nation, and its people are some of the poorest. In fact, Haiti is the poorest nation in the Americas.

More than USD two billion in aid has been fed into the country, but the crisis has not abated. Lawlessness still reigns. People are still homeless. About 1.5 million individuals have fled the capital to camps in other regions in an effort to rebuild their lives.

One such group of homeless people, comprising 25 families, has been living on a private block of land in the Lascahobas area. They were due to be evicted at the end of 2011.

Then a group of international organisations stepped in to set up a housing co-operative.

This group comprised the Housing Co-operative and Solidarity Mutual COLONSO and the Groupe d'Appui aux Rapatries et Refugies, the Americas Region of the International Co-operative Alliance (ICA), the Swedish Co-operative Centre and the Uruguayan Federation of Mutual Aid Housing Co-operatives. They laid the financial foundations for the local people to build on.

Yet the co-operative sector in Haiti suffers the same level of distrust as other Haitian institutions and public sector organisations. Misuse of funds has seen co-operatives struggle to prosper. As a result, only some credit co-operatives and agricultural co-operatives are still active.

As a nation, the Haitian people have much to be proud of. Haiti was the first country in Latin America and the Caribbean to win independence, and it became the first Black-led republic after a slave revolution in 1804. This history is a reminder for the Haitian people of what they can achieve against the odds.

BUCHAREST, ROMANIA

Romania has a long history of co-operation. Indeed, the first producer and service co-operative, the Society of Shoemakers, was founded in Bucharest in 1879.

Romania can also lay claim to being one of the founders of the International Co-operative Alliance (ICA).

Nearly two decades after the Society of Shoemakers was founded, Dimitrie C Butculescu – a cultured man, researcher and politician – was an honorary president of the founding congress of the ICA in 1895.

But it was not until 1951 that the first congress of handicraft co-operatives was held and the National Union of Handicraft and Production Co-operatives (UCECOM) founded.

"In the desert of the communist regime, handicraft co-operatives were an oasis of private capital, and they suffered many injustices," UCECOM writes.

The period between 1959 and 1962 was dire for the co-operatives, whose numbers shrank by 55 percent.

"About 440 handicraft co-operatives were transformed, without any compensation, into republican and local industry state enterprises," the association explains.

Following the Revolution of 1989, handicraft activities continued to run in almost all the nation's urban centres and throughout all economic classes.

These handicraft co-operatives produced industrial and consumer goods for the domestic market and export, and supplied a variety of services to the population. They continue to do so today.

These traditional activities include the production of folk art and artistic crafts that reflect the Romanian spirit.

CONGO

To survive, at least temporarily, in the Congo between 1996 and 2003, both adults and children took up arms. Many who did not do so voluntarily were forced to participate. War became their means of subsistence. Those who did not fight suffered starvation and displacement.

When war ended in 2003, the job of re-establishing basic food supplies and returning displaced people to work began.

The United Nations Food and Agriculture Organisation (FAO) stepped in as part of a program to reintegrate ex-combatants with the agricultural sector.

The Demobilized People's Association for Community Development was established by 15 women and 35 men, with a management committee, a board of directors and a general assembly that met once a year. Of the 50 members, 12 were fishermen and women, 26 were herders and 12 were farmers.

Under the program, the fishermen and women organised themselves into teams of two. Each received 150 metres of fishing net, four Coleman lamps, one fishing line, five ropes, two canoes, six hoisting poles, six pulleys and two poles to link the canoe hulls. Those in herding received a bicycle, goats, feed and veterinary products. Those in agriculture received axes, machetes, seed (either maize or groundnuts) and a bicycle.

Organised co-operatively, the farmers were able to use their bicycles for a taxi service, which then provided the income to buy land. The fishing groups kept 60 percent of the proceeds from their catches, and deposited the remaining 40 percent into their co-operative's bank account. The goat farmers pooled their skills and took turns caring for the goats. Any offspring became the property of the association.

The members' work has guaranteed food and seed supplies in their region, and the association is building its cash reserves to enable it to diversify its operations – for example, by opening a carpentry and sewing workshop.

Not only has the number of members doubled since the association was formed, but their standard of living has also risen. More importantly, there has been a collective realisation that these displaced people can take control of their own future without resorting to arms.

This story was made possible thanks to research by FAO personnel.

NIASSA, MOZAMBIQUE

Paulino Imede has seen the co-operative movement wax and wane in one of the world's poorest countries.

Niassa province, tucked in the northeast coast of Mozambique, the nation lying in the Indian Ocean in South East Africa, is this former Portuguese colony's poorest province.

After Mozambique's long battle for independence was won in 1975, Imede was one of the 75 farmers in Niassa who began, somewhat sceptically, to build an agricultural co-operative.

Mozambique had achieved independence thanks to the Marxist-based Liberation Front of Mozambique (FRELIMO). For the next 17 years, civil war raged between FRELIMO, backed by Cuba and the Soviet Union, and the Mozambican National Resistance (RENAMO) faction, supported by the white minority government in South Africa.

Farmers who had previously worked under a feudal landlord system were encouraged by the one-party state system to form co-operatives. The agricultural co-operative in Lussanhando was one of five established at the time.

At first, these co-operatives prospered. In 1983, the Lussanhando co-operative was hailed as a big success, winning accolades from Mozambique's President, Samora Machel. Its symbols of prosperity included a bicycle, a Mercedes-Benz truck and a farm tractor. Within two years, however, this co-operative was the last still operating as the intensifying guerrilla fighting halted farming. By 1985, Lussanhando had also ceased to operate.

It wasn't until the late 1980s, near the end of the civil war, that the new government recommenced its push to form co-operatives. Imede, with his primary school education, his two farms of corn, butter beans, peppers and potatoes, and his eight children, has remained at the forefront of the co-operative movement in Niassa.

LESOTHO

Khotso, pula, nala – peace, rain, prosperity – is the motto of the mountainous, landlocked kingdom of Lesotho.

After being colonised by the British, then fought over by the Boers and later by its own people, this diamond-rich highland country has been at peace since 1999. With 40 percent of its population living below the international poverty line and more than 30 percent suffering from AIDS, the means to prosperity is a key consideration. In addition to the diamond industry, Lesotho receives income from selling water to South Africa, the nation that surrounds it.

One legacy of British colonisation was the introduction of the co-operative business model. Pioneered in the 1940s, co-operatives have been part of the country's economic make-up ever since. There is broad-based acceptance of the co-operative model and its benefits by the population.

After years of strife, economic revival will be the key to a peaceful future for Lesotho, and the establishment of co-operative businesses may well help the nation to achieve that state. Today, even in schools, co-operatives are taking root in Lesotho. At Mohales Hoek High School, a student co-operative has existed since 2004.

Rise and Shine Student Co-operative was established to provide savings facilities and small loans to its members. Two of the biggest difficulties Lesotho youths face in attending school are paying the fees and buying a uniform. Without a school uniform, students are not allowed through the gates.

The co-operative has about 40 members aged between 15 and 21. In order to increase its capital base, the students have come up with a variety of innovative fundraising activities, including a chicken co-op, growing peaches and, perhaps most originally, a Mr & Miss Co-operative competition.

This story was made possible through research carried out by Sally Hartley (Co-operative College) for her doctoral studies.

DEIR KANOUN RAS EL EINS, LEBANON

The war of July 2006 decimated towns and villages in Lebanon. An estimated 1,200 people, mostly Lebanese, were killed in 34 days of fighting with Israeli forces. More than one million Lebanese citizens were displaced.

In the prosperous years before the war, Lebanon was known as the Switzerland of the East.

But in the south many villages were badly hit during the war. Some areas had to be abandoned because they were littered with Israeli land mines.

One town, Deir Kanoun Ras El Eins, had been home to a women's co-operative formed two years earlier. Started by 12 female members, the co-operative manufactured food products for the local community.

"After the 2006 war, the co-operative was almost destroyed, it was so damaged," remembers Daad Ismael, who runs the co-operative.

With the help of funds from the United Nations Development Program, the co-operative's members began to rebuild.

In Deir Kanoun Ras El Eins, a sesame bread called Mallet El Smeed is eaten. With the help of outside funding, the co-operative, by then 23 women strong, invested in commercial equipment. It now produces enough of the bread to distribute throughout Lebanon and to other countries.

"The co-operative is known all over Lebanon, in Beirut, in Tripoli," Ismael reports proudly. "The co-operative is also known in Tunis and Italy."

CHAPTER 2

*Healing abuse
and feeding the hungry*

KATHMANDU, NEPAL

Nepal is home to the world's tallest mountain, Everest, and one of the most magnificent natural environments in the world.

Yet in rural Nepal 81 percent of women are victims of domestic violence. On average, a woman is raped once every 54 minutes. Widows are termed *bokshi*, and are cast out as witches.

These travesties of human decency are widely tolerated, but not by Maheela, the local women's foundation, which was established in 1988. Maheela (which is also the Nepali word for women) founded a shelter for abused females and their children, and offered counselling, education and legal and human rights representation. It also set up a co-operative business arm.

Maheela's official name is Sakriya Adharshila Multi-Purpose Co-operative. Its woven products are sold around the world, and its members receive a 20 percent profit share as well as a salary. Funds earned from the co-operative also finance the shelter and the foundation's various activities, including those in the areas of education and microfinance.

Through Maheela, women who have been destitute find a way to support themselves. Women who have been outcast find acceptance and support. Women who have been abused find personal freedom.

LAKE ATITLÁN, GUATEMALA

Guatemala has the fourth highest rate of malnutrition in the world. Ninety percent of its indigenous people live in poverty and its indigenous children receive, on average, 1.3 years schooling.

Lake Atitlán lies in the remote Guatemalan highlands. The beauty of the lake and the three volcanoes guarding it is extraordinary, yet it stands in strong contrast with the poverty in which most of the surrounding indigenous people live.

Luisa Rosario Xicay Tacaxoy is head of the Artesanas Atitlán Co-operative in Santiago Atitlán, one of the indigenous people's villages by the lake. She has two children whom she adopted after a hurricane killed their parents. With her earnings from the co-operative, she has been able to send her children to school and build a brick-walled home for them.

In 2008, the Artesanas Atitlán Co-operative began working with the United States-based not-for-profit Mercado Global. Since then it has made jewellery for the giant Nordstrom department store chain in the USA.

By accepting Mercado Global's suggestion to incorporate its design expertise into their production process, Artesanas Atitlán Co-operative has been able to deliver greater returns to its members. Luisa earns three times more than she did before her relationship with Mercado Global began.

"This should allow mums to provide healthcare, send their kids to school, provide more nutritious foods for their families, improve their houses and also have savings," says Ruth DeGolia, the Executive Director of Mercado Global.

Photography Suzanne Becker Bronk

INDIA

"How many times do we need to prove that poor women are bankable?" wonders Jayshree Vyas, Managing Director of SEWA Bank.

This co-operative has proven that about 97 percent of its lenders meet their repayments – a better rate than any commercial bank in India.

The bank grew out of the needs of the poorest women in India, those who make their living picking rags, scavenging, vending vegetables or hand-rolling *bidis* (cigarettes).

It is owned by the all-female membership of the Self-Employed Women's Association (SEWA) and was established to help provide funding for women who would not be granted access to banking services. This helped some of its members to stop living in a debt trap, a situation in which many poor Indian women find themselves.

SEWA itself is a trade union, and is the one weapon the poorest female workers can use to protect themselves against more powerful economic forces. More than 1.2 million women have joined.

SEWA founder Elaben Bhatt has had some success in putting more power into the hands of these poor. The Gandhian practitioner of non-violence and self-reliance has significantly increased awareness of extreme poverty, both within India and overseas.

As Bhatt told a high-level session of the United Nations in 2008, "Poverty is powerlessness. Poverty cannot be removed unless the poor have power to make decisions that affect their lives."

ZAMBIA

"Strong voices are needed to advocate efforts to reduce rural poverty in line with the vision of turning the agricultural sector into the main engine of pro-poor growth."

– MAGGIE OKORE AND HANS PETER DEJGAARD, CONSULTANTS FOR THE SWEDISH CO-OPERATIVE CENTRE

Zambia – with about two-thirds of its population living in rural areas and the majority falling below the UN's extreme poverty line – needs solutions and strong voices. One of those voices is that of Jennifer Handondo, a member of the Zambia National Farmers Union.

Handondo joined the union in 1997. At that time she planted seedlings at her husband's farm and was, she says, a shy woman. A decade and a half later she had become a climate change activist and participated in the climate change talks in Durban in 2011.

Handondo, who credits the union with helping her to find her voice, has succeeded in gaining consultant work with aid organisations like World Vision.

She found the courage to leave her husband with nothing to her name. Now she has her own farm. She has her own consultancy. She has her freedom.

Standing behind Jennifer and others like her is the Zambia National Farmers Union. In little more than a decade this group of black, small landholders and white, commercial landholders has grown to become one of the most important and relevant farmers' organisations in southern Africa.

GUJARAT, INDIA

The state of Gujarat has much going for it. India's founding father, Mahatma Gandhi, came from this most western state of India. It boasts the fastest growing state economy in the nation and is one of India's most industrialised states.

Yet Gujarat's rapid industrialisation has caused small and marginal farmers in the Mehsana district to lose access to land. Excessive irrigation reduced the water table in the area, making water much more expensive. Local farmers were forced to seek casual work or to migrate elsewhere. Women farmers in this area were even harder hit.

The women organised themselves into the Vanlaxmi Women's Tree Growing Co-operative but struggled for two and a half years to regain access to land to farm. Then they happened upon a legal approach that delivered them the desired solution. By registering as a tree growers' co-operative rather than an agricultural co-operative, they were able to return to their land.

Once back on the land, the Vanlaxmi Women's Tree Growing Co-operative learnt how to maximise production with help from the

Gujarat Agriculture University. Using scientific agriculture practices including horticulture, agro-forestry, drip irrigation, compost pits and rainwater harvesting techniques, they improved the co-operative's operations significantly.

ABIDJAN, IVORY COAST

"I saw everyone – the government, local banks, international development organisations, even the World Bank. But no-one wanted to help us."

Rosalie Botti had done everything right. She and a group of other women had founded the Cocovico Vegetable Sellers Co-operative in the Ivory Coast's largest city, Abidjan. The co-operative expanded until it outgrew its squatted private land and needed a loan to move into commercial premises.

In stepped Oikocredit, one of the largest private lenders of microfinance to the developing world. Its objective was to lend money to local microfinance providers who, in turn, extended loans to the poor and disadvantaged, focusing on women and rural areas.

In the money-lending mainstream, Oikocredit is something of an enigma. Not being a bank, it has different priorities. While it stands for profit, it does not stand for profit maximisation.

When Oikocredit lent €700,000 to Cocovico in 2004, the Ivory Coast was still politically unstable. Civil war had broken out in Adibjan

two years earlier, and no-one else was lending. "Cocovico was a challenge for Oikocredit," says Mariam Dao, Oikocredit's West Africa Regional Director. "I love these kinds of challenges – investing in people, in poverty and seeing the reality that people can repay [the loans]."

After nearly 40 years of operation, Oikocredit has proven that lending money to applicants who have been rejected by the commercial banking system can be a successful business proposition.

The Cocovico Co-operative that Rosalie Botti founded is just one of 288 co-operatives that Oikocredit supports around the world.

FINLAND

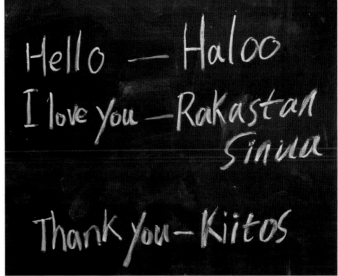

'Osuuskunta Toivo' means hope in Finnish – an appropriate name for an organisation that brings light to the lives of many Finnish children and their families.

This politically and religiously non-aligned health and social care co-operative emerged in 1997, above all from the desire of a handful of voluntary sector workers to create a workplace without bureaucracy.

Osuuskunta Toivo runs children's programs with names like Laku, a sweet Finnish liquorice. These programs have brought optimism to the lives of children aged between four and six with simultaneous behavioural and emotional disturbances. They have also delivered hope to children between the ages of seven and 12 who have neuropsychiatric problems and psychiatric disturbances.

Eero Riikonen, a psychiatrist and member of Osuuskunta Toivo, says these disturbances can be attributed, in part, to the strict Lutheran culture that lingers on in Finland. Children were traditionally part of a learning environment that drew attention to personal and employment problems.

Another program, Voimala ('Powerhouse'), works with children aged between five and 15 with psycho-social problems, and addresses their families and social networks.

In a country where an estimated 20 percent of the adult population consumes too much alcohol, Osuuskunta Toivo specialises in helping those who are down and out. Its Consultation Centre for Work Life specialises in work-related difficulties.

In Finland, family and work dominate everyday life, so rejection from family or work structures can be tremendously isolating. The work that the social workers, psychologists, neuropsychologists, doctors and teachers at Osuuskunta Toivo have done to rescue such individuals has won it great respect in healthcare and community circles. Only a handful of other organisations do anything remotely similar in the areas of child psychiatry, the rehabilitation of children and families, and youth employment.

COOP
STORE

This page: Arctic Co-operatives Limited, Canada.
Right: ReCoop, Malta.

CHAPTER 3

Starting new lives

SOUS VALLEY, MOROCCO

In the 17th century, the Sous Valley (Tamazirt n Sus in the local Berber language) was the wealthiest place in the prosperous Tazerwalt Kingdom. It was a centre for the gold and sugar trade for Dutch, English and Portuguese merchants.

Khadija Almadi and Khadija Idmoulay are two women living in this remote but fertile valley in southern Morocco.

"I am a widow and I need to meet my financial needs," says Almadi, who has six children.

Idmoulay has similar obligations and requirements. "I am a widow with two children who both need to be taken care of," she says.

Before the birth of a women's co-operative, these Berber women, disadvantaged by their lack of Arabic language and constrained by religious lifestyles, could not work to support their children. But the arrival of a PhD candidate from the Massachusetts Institute of Technology in the United States changed their future. Zahir Dossa, a student of development, realised he had the opportunity to do

what few of his colleagues had done. He could help Berber women establish a business to improve their lives.

The valley's savannah remains home to the endemic Argan tree, which grows a fruit containing a precious oil that can be used in both food and skin care. Thanks to Zahir Dossa's initiative, Argan Tree Co-operative has been established, bringing economic benefits to the entire Sous Valley through its 18 women members, all of whom conduct their trade via the internet.

"For every dollar you spend, 33 cents goes back to the producers. You know where your money goes," the co-operative boasts.

SHARJAH, UNITED ARAB EMIRATES

Um Ahmed's fingers work quickly, twisting and plaiting the palm leaf into sturdy shapes. Her hands, painted intricately with henna, are accustomed to making traditional food cover cones from brightly coloured fronds.

"I am proud to say that, as a United Arab Emirates (UAE) woman, I have a variety of skills," she says.

Um Ahmed has been given the opportunity to put her skills to work through a new co-operative program in Sharjah, one of the seven United Arab Emirates. "I believe that women should also take part in contributing to a household's income," she declares. "It is unfair to place the burden only on men."

Sharjah is proud of its credentials as the cultural centre of the United Arab Emirates. Boasting 17 museums, the United Nations Educational, Scientific and Cultural Organisation (UNESCO) has declared the state to be Arabia's cultural capital.

After a visit to the eastern and central regions of the emirates, HH Sheikha Jawaher Al Qasimi, the wife of the ruler of Sharjah,

saw the need to support women who keep traditional arts and crafts alive.

Um Ahmed shares HH Sheikha Jawaher Al Qasimi's ambition. "I would love to export our handicrafts outside the UAE, which is heavily reliant on imported goods," she says.

To help her do so, Sharjah Women's Business Council, together with the British-based charity Oxfam, established the Intilaqah Co-operative. Its aim was to promote entrepreneurship among the Emirate's female population.

The co-operative began in December 2011 with 50 members, and more are being encouraged to join. New members start by producing a feasibility study for their business idea and later receive advice on how to get the business started.

Um Ahmed says, "I always tell my children and daughters-in-law to learn these skills when they have free time."

BENIN

Women in Benin stand out in their beautifully designed, brightly coloured fabrics, but their clothing is one of the few areas of their lives in which they have freedom of choice. In this tropical sliver of West Africa, women are traditionally subservient to men.

In 1993, the Benin country director for the Boston-based NGO (non-governmental organisation) World Education – itself founded by a remarkable woman, Welthy Honsinger Fisher – initiated a program together with the US Agency for International Development (USAID) to assist women to organise co-operatives.

After seeing the success of mothers' associations in neighbouring Burkina Faso, Al Miller of World Education organised a delegation to visit some of these co-operatives. The group included female government representatives, NGO representatives and one woman representing a parent-teacher association.

This delegation found that in Burkina Faso mothers' associations operated independently of the male-dominated parent-teacher associations. It was decided that this would

not be the best option in Benin, due to the risk of antagonism between women and men. However, Benin's first mothers' associations began with only women members.

This initiated a chain reaction. The women began to flourish in their new-found freedom and empowerment. The men, witnessing the energy of the women organised co-operatively, afforded them more respect. Women and men began to work collaboratively. Girls began to go to school.

"The women want their daughters to be educated," says Shirley Burchfield, Vice-President of World Education's Africa division. "Any opportunity to improve their girls' schooling, and they're willing to jump in there and do it."

Now, nearly 20 years on, there are 630 mothers' associations in Benin operating across 749 schools.

The true test of these mothers' associations has been how they perform after their development funding has been discontinued. In Benin they have thrived, and now so do their daughters.

WASHINGTON STATE, USA

Alice Turtle Robb blogs. Alice Turtle Robb writes novels. Alice Turtle Robb wonders about the connection between independence, intimacy, dignity and … toileting.

Alice Turtle Robb is a caregiver.

Alice Turtle Robb is also a member, owner and the chairperson of the Circle of Life Co-operative in Whatcom County, Washington State. She cares for elders, many of whom have dementia; people she refers to as her "Heart Song" folk.

Alice Turtle Robb writes of coming to grips with the awfulness of dementia, although, she counsels, the reality is not always awful. She is one of about a dozen caregivers who shop for, wash, clean and, most importantly, communicate with these folks.

For this caregiver, it is not hard. She says she has been blessed with a genetic form of optimism. She makes light work of chaos, finds dignity in awfulness.

But it was not just the Pollyanna traits of its caregivers that helped Circle of Life turn its first profit in 2011. It was the fact that

Circle of Life caregivers are also co-op members. Think of it as a circle of care.

CUMBRIA, UNITED KINGDOM

Early in 2011 a group of about 100 residents of the Cumbrian village of Crosby Ravensworth, in the Lakes District's Lyvennet Valley, gathered in the village hall. At issue was the impending closure of the parish's only remaining pub, the Butchers Arms.

In the hall that night a vote was taken to save the pub. A co-operative was formed, a purchase offer was made and a process was set in motion to strengthen community life in the village.

The £255,000 offer was accepted in March 2011, and the newly formed co-operative was given until June of that year to gather the funds. By 7 June, around £300,000 had been raised from 297 members including the local Member of Parliament – enough to buy the property and to refurbish it.

Little more than two months later, British Prime Minister David Cameron came to the pub for 'lunch and a chat'. The PM was the first to sign the pub's visitor book.

Ten days after that the pub, which had been renamed Lyvennet Community Pub, was officially opened. Jetting in for the event was a co-operative member from Australia. John Stubbs had grown up in the pub between 1958 and 1978, when his family owned it. When he heard back home in Australia that the co-operative was looking for members and funds, he offered to help out.

These days you have to book a table if you want to eat at the pub on the weekends. Tuesday night is musicians' night, Thursday lunchtime is a lunch club for senior members of the parish, and on Friday nights the village's schoolchildren drop in for a cola.

Food is sourced by the pub's kitchen from local cattle and sheep farmers.

The village pub lives on.

EASTERN DZONGKHAGS, BHUTAN

Lemongrass is a spiky grass that grows wild in the mountainous kingdom of Bhutan. In some countries, lemongrass is believed to guard against anxiety, in others to help with coughs.

Paradoxically, Bhutanese people themselves don't ingest it. The value of lemongrass for the people of the kingdom is in the oil that can be distilled from it and marketed for export.

The Lemongrass Co-operative in Bhutan's eastern Dzongkhags, or regions, had been operating as a co-operative even before it was officially registered in 2011. Its 170 members, more than 70 percent of them women, had been working together informally to distil and sell lemongrass oil since 2007.

The co-operative exports its product through a business called Bio Bhutan, which manufactures soap and other products using the special oil. It also exports oil to neighbouring India, Nepal and Thailand.

The kingdom's Ministry of Economic Affairs has run the Essential Oils Development Program since 1993. The program assists in building the lemongrass manufacturing industry in the remote eastern regions. The Department of Cottage and Small Industry in the Ministry of Economic Affairs provides the necessary marketing resources.

Profit margins are higher than in many other industries in Bhutan, so for those living in hillside villages in the country's east, lemongrass oil manufacture is the best business to be in.

PENNSYLVANIA, USA

Casey Spacht was one of nine farmers who met on a Saturday afternoon in 2006 in a barn in Lancaster County, Pennsylvania.

Feeling exploited by middlemen, these farmers were, among other things, trying to find a way to hold out against commercial pressures to farm with chemicals. As Spacht put it, "We were wanting to take the power back and reclaim our lives".

Many of the farmers present that day were from Amish farming families with small landholdings, who lived without electricity, telephones and cars. No-one had money to splash around. Working with a small grant, the farmers hired a driver, renovated an old granary as an office and rented a small warehouse space with refrigeration. In what has been nicknamed Pennsylvania Dutch Country, the Lancaster Farm Fresh Co-operative, a non-profit organic farmers' co-op, was born.

For Spacht, the co-operative was "like a new, extended family that [he] never had". Raised in a broken home, his father a heroin addict, his mother depressed and addicted to over-the-counter painkillers, Spacht had later worked with a natural food co-operative and lived in a housing co-operative. Lancaster Farm Fresh Co-operative, with a marketing arm for its Amish farmers, was a natural progression.

"No need for multinational corporations, no need for harmful technologies in the name of progress," remembers Spacht. "Just love for the land, love for our families and extending that into our community to create a wider web."

The Amish and non-Amish farming families advised each other on what to grow and how to plant, harvest, grade and pack. This created numerous jobs in the community, all within 150 miles of where the crops were grown.

The co-operative has 80 member farmers and supports at least 100 farmers through the year through its marketing, sales and online shop. Starting with just nine farmers in 2006, the co-operative grew nine-fold over the next six years.

And Spacht's farm, Lancaster Farmacy, is behind what is known as a community-supported medicine share, which grows herbs, makes herbal remedies and distributes them throughout the community.

"It's a way for me to farm, but also a way to get back at the drug culture that tore my family apart," says Spacht. "Educating people about taking care of their body correctly, and not relying on synthetic remedies with harmful side effects."

Spacht and his fellow co-operative members have taken their power back.

GHANA, LIBERIA, KENYA AND UGANDA

Football, association football or soccer – call it what you will – is the world's most popular sport. One of the world's best football clubs, FC Barcelona, is owned by its members and run on co-operative principles.

This proves that the co-operative model works at the top end of the sport. And a growing network of co-operative football clubs is demonstrating that the model also works at grassroots level in Africa. Through a network known as Sandlanders Football, the global community can become associate members of four different co-operative football clubs in Ghana, Liberia, Kenya and Uganda.

Keta Sandlanders in Ghana, Ligi Ndogo SSC in Kenya, VOA Sandlanders in the Liberian capital of Monrovia, and Mutundwe Sandlanders in Uganda make up the Sandlanders network.

"The network is growing and will soon include a number of other clubs from across Africa that already have a strong tradition of community ownership of sports clubs," says Sandlanders' co-founder, Paul Jones.

The clubs have all come from humble beginnings. To establish Mutundwe Sandlanders, the founder, Chris Kalibbala, ran a succession of Nsolo Nnene (big animal) and Nsolo Ntono (small animal) football competitions. Participants played for the first seven years on an abandoned building site. When the building works were revived, the football side was homeless until a local family helped out by providing new land.

In typical co-operative fashion, Sandlanders clubs involve themselves in projects that benefit their local communities. Mutundwe Sandlanders is providing a venue in Kampala, the nation's capital, where talented players from all over Uganda can improve their skills.

Meanwhile, at Keta Sandlanders, club members are working on plans to develop a new community centre and playing field.

TERRACE, CANADA

It's not often that individuals can boast that they own a ski hill, but members of My Mountain Co-op, the first non-profit community ski co-operative in Canada, have every right to do so.

The co-operative recently purchased Shames Mountain Ski Area, near Terrace in northwest British Columbia (BC). Shames Mountain is not just any ski hill. Blessed with more than 40 feet of snow every winter, it has the highest annual snowfall of any lift-serviced resort in North America, producing what the members like to call 'legendary skiing'.

But northwest BC is generally known for its forestry and fishing industries, which had been declining for more than 10 years. So when Shames' original corporate owners wanted to retire and sell the ski area, no buyers were forthcoming.

Following two years of research by a group of locals wanting to maintain an operational ski hill, My Mountain Co-op was born. In November 2011, after eight months of fundraising, the co-operative bought Shames Mountain. To date almost a thousand local, regional and international individuals and businesses have purchased memberships, thereby investing in the future of Shames Mountain and northwest BC.

The co-operative is doing well, say the members. During its first year of operation it garnered support from the communities of Prince Rupert, Kitimat, Terrace and local schools. It has also received donations from many businesses, including the Prince Rupert Port Authority and one of the world's largest mining companies, Rio Tinto Alcan. A new snow-grooming machine has been purchased, and lift and infrastructure improvements will be completed in summer 2012.

Fortunately for its members, Shames Mountain lived up to its reputation in winter 2011/2012, delivering some of the best skiing that local 'powder hounds' can remember. With a recent surge in industrial development in northwest BC, the future of My Mountain Co-op remains bright.

MALTA

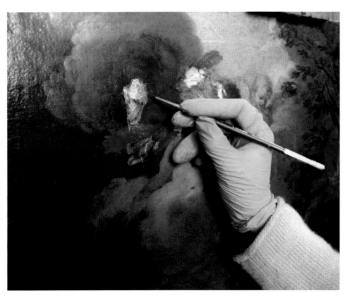 

For a team of art lovers, restoration work is a source of major satisfaction. "One starts off with a filthy wall with dirt and surface damage which, as it is being documented, studied and conserved, finds its way back to its strengthened and uncovered original splendour," explains Agatha Grima, Director of the co-operative ReCoop (Restoration and Conservation Co-op Ltd).

ReCoop was set up in 2003 by a team of professional conservators wanting to work in the arts sector. At that time professional conservation was in its infancy on the Maltese Islands, so the co-operative made a priority of educating the public about their work, offering public lectures when projects were completed.

What began as a team of conservators grew into a multidisciplinary group including art historians, architects and scientists. Apart from conservation and restoration services, the team offers historical and scientific art research, environmental monitoring and consultancy services.

"Maybe the most important moments in ReCoop's evolution were when it won major projects for the conservation of the bastions of Valletta, Birgu, Mdina and the Citadel Gozo," says Grima. "These projects have given a new dimension to the co-operative."

ReCoop has worked on numerous projects, ranging from easel paintings to bronze and wooden poly-chromed statues, wall paintings and architectural monuments.

Among its most important projects have been the restoration of the Carmelite church and convent and numerous projects at St. John's Cathedral. The team's latest work is on the painted ceiling at the Mdina Cathedral, while other recent works include the altar painting of Stella Maris church, Sliema.

"The team started off as a group of professional conservators, but suddenly they had to take on the role of managers," says Grima. "The fact that one could follow pre-defined co-operative structures definitely eased the task of the founding members.

"As the co-operative grew and embraced new members, the co-operative structure worked for ReCoop, because ReCoop is a multidisciplinary team that functions with one common aim – preserving cultural heritage."

USA; CANADA

Coffee is the most important export of the tropical nations of the world, and the primary export of a number of developing countries.

When Bill Harris walked through the door of a coffee farmers' co-operative in the highlands Chiapas region of Mexico, he met Monika Firl who was working there. Later, following many conversations about fair trade and the best way to support small-scale coffee farmers, the importer Co-operative Coffees was established, followed by a sister organisation, CoopSol.

Today, Co-operative Coffees is owned by its 24 roaster members throughout the USA and Canada.

"We expect to purchase 3.5 million pounds of green coffee in 2012, or an estimated USD11 million in contracts paid directly to small-farmer co-operatives," says Monika Firl, now Co-operative Coffees' producer relations manager. "In the coffee industry this makes us a small player – which motivates us all the more to make every gesture count.

"We strive for maximum, positive impact on the lives of small-scale farmers – whom we consider to be the backbone of this industry – as well as creating positive impact at every subsequent step along the way."

Co-operative Coffees is passionate about the changes that have taken place in the fair trade movement. The new Fair Trade For All campaign, set up by Fair Trade USA under its former name TransFair USA, broke away from the Fair Trade Labelling Organization, enabling plantation coffee producers to receive their accreditation.

Yet, as Firl explains, ethical labour conditions on coffee plantations do not themselves ensure fairness. The best way to improve the living conditions of poor farmers, she believes, is to support them by trading directly with them rather than with the big plantations.

"At Co-operative Coffees, we don't believe in trickle-down economics," says Firl. "If channelling resources through the most consolidated centres of power was functional, we would not be in this worldwide economic mess to begin with. We believe that change happens when you empower the disadvantaged and marginalised."

ARCTIC, CANADA
ARCTIC CO-OPERATIVES LIMITED

There is an Inuit phrase, 'A long time ago, in the future'. In other words, we must look at our history to understand where we are going. The history of co-operatives in the Arctic tells a compelling story of what ordinary people can accomplish by working together.

The first community-owned and controlled Arctic co-operatives were incorporated in 1959. Setting up a local co-operative was often seen as a way to support the traditional way of life. Arts and crafts production, fur harvesting and commercial fisheries are examples of cultural activities that were the basis of early co-operatives in the north. The co-operative model of working together is strikingly parallel to the values and natural approach of Arctic communities. Early leaders were visionaries, and members understood the value of pooling resources and working together to 'build a better world through co-operative enterprise'.

Co-operative members have had to overcome a great many challenges – harsh environmental conditions, the remoteness of communities, limited access to services and significant changes to their traditional way of life. Inuit and Dené people in the Canadian Arctic adapted to change and overcame adversity – a true reflection of a resilient and spirited people.

Andy Morrison, CEO, Arctic Co-operatives Limited (ACL) explains, "Although the first limited contact the aboriginal people of the Northwest Territories and Nunavut had with other cultures took place over 300 years ago when European explorers ventured into the Canadian Arctic, change began to happen very quickly for the Inuit, Dené and Métis people of the Arctic about 50 years ago when health and education services were started in many areas."

Communities developed and people whose lifestyle had been nomadic for thousands of years started to move to the locations where services were available.

Legal businesses were formed and co-operatives became the first locally owned and controlled business enterprises within those communities.

"When the people of Nunavut and Northwest Territories started to establish rudimentary settlements," says Morrison, "they did exactly what they did when living on the land – they supported each other and helped each other; they co-operated."

In 2012 ACL celebrates the 40th anniversary of the incorporation of the first service federation of co-operatives in the Arctic. In February 1972, delegates from 26 co-operatives met in Churchill, Manitoba, to discuss the benefits of working together through a co-operative service federation. One common thread holding these 26 co-operatives together was pride in the ownership of their new community-owned and controlled businesses. Not only were they proud of the services and benefits they provided to their communities, they were also very proud of their autonomy and independence.

Today there are 31 co-operatives in communities throughout Nunavut and the Northwest Territories, representing the interests of thousands of members, providing jobs and marketing arts and crafts, furs and country foods. Co-operatives in the Arctic are involved in general merchandise retailing, hotels, contracting, taxi and cartage services, commercial fisheries, bakeries and cable television services.

ACL is a service federation providing essential support services to its 31 community-based member co-operatives located throughout Canada's Arctic. The primary role of the federation is to co-ordinate the resources and combined purchasing power of these co-operatives as they work together to ensure the ongoing social and economic advancement of their communities.

Arctic Co-operatives Limited

"Luchamos por una Patria socialmente Justa económicamente libre y políticamente soberana."

Evita.

1952-26 de Julio-2009

Para los compañe de la **UST** el compromiso que los chicos s los privilegiado ayer, hoy y sie

This page: Artes Gráfica Chilavert, Argentina.
Right: Kuapa Kokoo Co-operative, Ghana.
Photography Kim Naylor

CHAPTER 4

Empowering workers

CHILAVERT, ARGENTINA

On a wall of the Spanish colonial-style villa in Argentina that houses the small printing co-operative, Artes Gráfica Chilavert, is a section of unfinished brickwork surrounded by a picture frame. This patch of masonry is a reminder to the co-operative's 14 members that they must continue to fight to keep their business alive.

The financial depths into which Argentina plummeted in 2001 marked an all-time low for the printing firm Artes Gráfica Chilavert. Its employees had already worked months of unpaid hours. Since the 1980s, the firm's silver-tongued proprietor had convinced his staff that financial salvation was always just around the corner, promising new, bigger machines and much larger contracts. Meanwhile he was selling off its assets and reinvesting nothing.

Finally, in April 2002, the employer told the eight remaining workers, who had survived years of downsizing, that he had never intended to buy new machines. "Don't you see what situation the country is in?" he asked them disingenuously. The following day the staff decided to fight to keep their jobs.

So began their occupation of the printing works. With the help of the surrounding community, which fed them and provided bedding and physical support, the workers maintained their vigil over the machines.

On 24 May, when the workers received their first eviction notice, there were eight police cars, eight assault vehicles, two ambulances and a fire truck outside the building. Keeping these authorities at bay were about 300 community members who camped outside the printing works.

During their occupation the workers maintained their spirits by printing their first book as a co-operative, a collection of essays by well-known and progressive Argentinean thinkers.

They smuggled copies of the book out through a hole they burrowed through the brick wall and into a neighbouring house. From there the books were loaded into a car boot and driven to market, under the noses of the police who had guarded the printing works for several months.

This story was made possible with the assistance and research of European Research Institute on Cooperative and Social Enterprises (Euricse) research fellow Marcelo Vieta.

LUZON, PHILIPPINES

When Spanish conquistadores landed at the southern end of the island of Luzon in 1576, the *haciendas* (rural estates) and *encomiendas* (legal systems) they established marked the beginning of land dispossession for millions of people in the Philippines.

More than 400 years later, following the 'people power revolution' that ousted the dictatorship of Ferdinand Marcos, a Philippine farmer named Pablito Dante set in motion a series of events that would finally deliver agrarian reform to Luzon, one of the three largest islands in the Philippines.

Pablito founded the Pecuaria Development Co-operative, which recovered 800 hectares of agricultural land under the agrarian reform program.

Pablito stood firm during the lengthy negotiations required before the farmers' co-operative became owner and operator of the land. Ultimately, it cost him his life. Illegal farmer-entrants murdered him in a violent land grab.

But Dante's death inspired his fellow members to continue their struggle for ownership against rival farmers – and government red tape – for another three years.

In 1993 their dream was realised. Miller, the new co-operative's manager, pushed hard to ensure complete security of their landholding.

Houses for the co-operative members were built on the land, even though there were no roads and it was not connected to electricity or water supplies.

For the next decade Miller and his brother worked to find the best organic rice seed. This led them to build a bio-organic fertiliser processing plant and a rice mill, resulting in a greater market share. Today, having captured nearly half the national market, Pecuaria-produced red and brown rice is one of the bestselling brands in the Philippines.

SUMILAO, PHILIPPINES

The march lasted 73 days and crossed 1,700km.

In late 2007 a group of landless Lumad (indigenous peoples with Higaonon ancestry from the Philippine island of Mindanao) set out from Sumilao to the Philippine capital of Manila, capturing the nation's attention.

The seriousness with which the government of Gloria Macapagal-Arroyo eventually treated this protest was revealed at a meeting with the farmers in the president's palace, when a revocation order was issued allowing the farmers to reclaim their land.

During the two decades these Sumilao farmers had been fighting for land reform, they had twice been granted ownership of their 144 hectares of ancestral land, only to see it revoked and returned to the previous landowner each time.

Not surprisingly, the land reform legislation that finally allowed them to return faced strong opposition in parliament, led by no less than the President's brother-in-law.

Yet this was not the group's first non-violent protest. Ten years earlier, 17 of the farmers had staged a 28-day hunger strike in front of the Department of Agrarian Reform in Quezon City to pressure the government.

Their fight had its roots in the agrarian reform of the Philippines, undertaken with limited success following the ousting of dictator Ferdinand Marcos in 1986. At that time a plan was hatched to restore a third of the country's land to its rightful owners. Two decades later, about 75 percent of it had been returned.

However, these farmers had no access to capital, irrigation or marketing. About a quarter of them had to sell or mortgage their farms. Most were living below the poverty line. Those who formed co-operative structures fared better than others.

Pablito Dante, the murdered co-founder of Percuaria Development Co-operative (featured elsewhere in this book) was the inspiration for this group of landless farmers. Their leader, Rene Penas, was later to suffer the same terrible fate as Dante for his convictions.

The Pecuaria co-operative members supported the Sumilao farmers' protests as best they could. They fed and entertained them, helping to keep their spirits up and their resolve high. Eventually, the movement achieved its ultimate objective. In 2009 the Philippine President signed a law to see the agrarian reforms finally enacted.

And once the Sumilao land was officially designated a co-operative holding, it was the fellow co-operators of Pecuaria who provided the Sumilao co-op farmers with advice.

BEIJING, CHINA

On New Zealander Rewi Alley's 80th birthday, Chinese leader Deng Xiaoping described him as "our veteran fighter, old friend and comrade".

Few foreigners have played as significant a role in China as Alley. He was the father of the nation's industrial co-operatives. In a sense, Alley had been groomed from an early age for the work he would come to do. His parents were both teachers. His mother was a suffragette and his father spent his last 20 years working for rural co-operatives. After fighting in World War I, Alley tried to make a go of farming in recession-hit New Zealand. After six years of struggle, he travelled to Shanghai in 1927. It was while working as a chief factory inspector that his eyes were opened to the appalling conditions in Chinese factories.

The Japanese invasion of China a decade later gave Alley the opportunity to do something about what he had seen. He founded the International Committee for the Promotion of Chinese Industrial Co-operatives (ICCIC). The Chinese name for 'China Industrial Co-operatives' was Zhongguo Gongye Hezhoushe, abbreviated to Gong He and then to Gung Ho. Alley served as the ICCIC's Secretary, and Madame Soong Ching Ling, the widow of the Chinese revolutionary and President Sun Yat-sen, was President. Within two years, more than 30,000 members were working in 3,000 co-operatives in 16 Chinese provinces.

But the Gung Ho co-operatives had dwindled by the 1950s, and their profiles were further reduced during China's Cultural Revolution between 1966 and 1976.

It was not until government reforms were introduced that Alley, then 85, revived the movement. Grassroots co-operatives began to spring up in Beijing where Alley lived; Hubei, where he had worked in flood relief in the 1930s; and Shandan, where he had sited his school in the 1940s.

Gung Ho has since gone on to work with the World Bank, national co-operative associations and NGOs to establish more Chinese co-operatives.

Portrait of Rewi Alley (acrylic on hessian on board, 900mm x 900mm) by New Zealand artist Rudolf Boelee.

CÓRDOBA, ARGENTINA

December 2001: The Argentine economy is in ruins, the peso-dominated bank accounts of its middle classes have been frozen, yet the foreign-denominated bank accounts of its wealthy elite have not been touched.

Downtown in Córdoba, Argentina's second-largest city, a private medical clinic is on its last legs after the doctor owners have cleaned out its funds, leaving nurses and staff unpaid.

So began an ownership tale that would see the Clínica Junín medical clinic pass through a series of owners and ghost companies while its medical services were reduced to almost zero.

The clinic's employees, who had no hope of finding other jobs, decided to run the clinic as a co-operative. For many of the female nurses there was no other option – their husbands had lost their jobs in the economic collapse, and they had become their families' sole breadwinners.

For veteran nurse Ana María Barrionuevo, whose marriage crumbled during this upheaval, it was the support she received from outsiders that kept her going as she moved, first into the homes of relatives, then into rundown rental rooms.

"When we took the clinic, none of us had a single cent in our pockets. And suddenly these young people from several left wing political parties, social movements and from the university said they would help us with our strike fund," she recalls. "It was really not much money, but at the time it seemed like a lot to us … It is what kept us going, what gave us the energy in those early days to keep fighting for this."

A decade later, the co-operative is the fastest growing medical clinic in the province.

"We managed to transform this place from the bottom up. I'm talking about everything here that relates to affordable healthcare delivery," explains Alejandro Torres, a co-founder and treasurer of the co-operative. "We don't overcharge for coming to our clinic. A lot of people think because you pay more, you get better service.

This is not correct. Charging more and privatising health is really about making a profit; it is not really about caring for patients. We have shown that you can offer health service at an affordable rate, an accessible rate, and that everyone has a right to health."

This story was made possible with the assistance and research of European Research Institute on Cooperative and Social Enterprises (Euricse) postdoctoral research fellow Marcelo Vieta.

TVER, RUSSIA

In Russia in the late 1990s, the rouble had collapsed and some factory workers were paid in pickles. These were really hard years.

Svetlana Maksimova and her family were forced to sell their flat and move to the forest where they lived in a trailer. They did not have sufficient money to buy feed for their animals. "It was wintertime and I milked the cows myself," she recalls.

Later, when their farmhouse burnt down, Maksimova had to apply for an emergency loan to rebuild it. With the help of the community, she managed to do so. "People were happy [to help] as we produced organic food," she says.

To make her produce available to as many people as possible, Maksimova decided to set up a farmers' co-operative union. "It was frustrating that farmers had no way to deliver their produce to the consumer," she remembers. "The issue was that farmers had no access to the market; it was controlled by big companies.

"So we came up with the idea of setting up special logistics centres and joining the farmers together in co-operatives.

The farmers could deliver their produce to be processed at the centres and at weekends we would arrange food fairs. The farmers were sure they'd be able to provide everybody with safe and nutritious food."

In November 2011 the farmer's union, which by then had 500 members, nominated Maksimova to run for office in the state elections. She is now a deputy in the State Duma and the head of the Tver region of the Farmers and Smallholders Association to Moscow's north.

While Makisoma sits in the Duma, her daughter runs the farm.

This story was made possible with the assistance of Oxfam's Becky Wynn and other staff.

KUMASI, GHANA

Elias Mohammed is 'the Recorder'.

More than 10 years ago he was simply another Ghanaian cocoa farmer taking whatever price he could get from the local cocoa-buying company and being paid late or inadequately. Being cheated at the scales was an occupational hazard.

That was until he and 20 of his fellow farmers decided to join the Kuapa Kokoo Co-operative.

Ever since, Elias Mohammed has held the job of attending the scales, recording the weight of farmers' cocoa bean production in his district, and keeping an eye on quality. His fellow farmers rate him so highly they elected him to the national executive committee that heads the organisation.

Fairness permeates everything Kuapa Kokoo does. The co-operative receives a Fairtrade price for its cocoa and, unlike many other farmer co-operatives throughout the world, it also takes a portion of the profits of the marketing company Divine Chocolate, in which it owns a 45 percent share.

Divine Chocolate reaps profits from the sale of chocolate and other products made from the bags of cocoa beans Elias produces and those supplied by more than 65,000 cocoa farmer members of Kuapa Kokoo.

Photography Kim Naylor

VILLA DOMÍNICO, ARGENTINA

This is the story of 34 workers who turned the tables on Techint, Argentina's largest multinational company.

In the late 1990s Techint was involved in more than 100 businesses around the world, but the thorn in its side was a waste disposal business in its home patch in Villa Domínico, just south of Buenos Aires.

In Techint's Buenos Aires' boardrooms, executives were working out how to reduce the number of workers in the business. Before their strategies could be implemented, the resulting bad publicity convinced Techint to exit the business altogether.

The workers responded by forming a worker co-operative called UST (Unión Solidaria de Trabajadores, or Workers' Solidarity Union) to revitalise their business. They then applied themselves to realising a dream that was an anathema to their former employer – they transformed an industrial eyesore into an ecological green belt. The workers expanded the co-operative's activities, creating new jobs and starting many new community development projects. UST members stabilised the co-operative's revenue by securing state waste management contracts. This enabled UST to invest 25 percent of its revenue in establishing a range of community assets including a high school, a health clinic, a sports centre, a community bank, a waste recycling program and a multimedia centre – all of them co-operatives.

"We workers can take our destiny in our own hands," proclaims one of UST's promotional brochures. The co-operative's softly spoken leader, Mario Barrios (one of 34 original members, who now number 90), describes the UST even more eloquently. "For us it is satisfying to be able to say that we workers aren't only capable of managing ourselves," he says. They are also "putting policies and procedures into place that are friendly to the environment, and doing community work. At the UST, we aren't just thinking about making a profit."

This story was made possible by the assistance and research of European Research Institute on Cooperative and Social Enterprises (Euricse) research fellow Marcelo Vieta.

ULAANBAATAR AND GOVI-ALTAI, MONGOLIA

As Altantuya tells the story, the co-operative movement in Mongolia grew out of the communist regime.

"Our organisation was initially founded in 1967 in the socialist regime – we were called 'The Supreme Council of Cooperatives'," she explains.

Altantuya, the head of the International Cooperation Department at the National Association of Mongolian Agricultural Cooperatives (NAMAC), said what had been called collective farms under the Soviet regime were later reorganised into co-operatives. "After the democratic changes in 1990, half of them reorganised into co-operatives," she explained. "In 1992, they had their first general assembly and then they re-established the association as NAMAC."

However, the move to co-operation has thrown up its own challenges. "Still now in Mongolia we are faced with false co-operatives," laments Altantuya. Nevertheless, NAMAC has expanded to include 22 offices managing the affairs of 460 primary co-operative members and eight secondary co-operative members.

One of those members is Undral, a collective farm that became a co-operative 36 years after its inception. Part of its operations were privatised, but its real estate formed part of the new co-operative in the remote Dariv *soum* (or township) of Govi-Altai province.

At a distance of 280km from the closest regional centre and about 1,400km from the Mongolian capital of Ulaanbaatar, the co-operative has set out to be an economic centre for the region. It provides micro-loans to its farmer members and purchases their livestock, as well as providing consumer goods.

In spite of its remote location and the region's lack of development, Undral has become the largest and most powerful rural co-operative in Mongolia.

JARGALANT SOUM, MONGOLIA

What do four single mothers do when the government unit they worked in is privatised and their jobs are eroded?

In the case of these four women, they decided to grow their own business, a co-operative business.

"After the privatisation of the forestry unit, we were dismissed in 1998 and it has become very difficult for us to survive," explains D. Tsendsuren.

The four linked up with six other single mothers and together established Ur Jims, which means Fruit Co-operative, in 1998. Located in Jargalant *soum* (township) in the Khovd province, the co-operative is in one of the most remote regions in Mongolia, more than 1,500km from the capital, Ulaanbaatar.

For the first four years, the 10 women worked for no salary and each contributed start-up capital to the business of 250,000 tugrugs, or about USD 200.

Twelve years later the co-operative's capital base had increased to 85 million tugrugs.

Taking the best from their former careers, the women have made as their goal the reforestation of their remote region. With 90 percent of Mongolia's vast lands vulnerable to desertification they began with a plan to reforest one hectare of land, planting 56,000 tree saplings. Without any spare cash in the business to purchase fencing materials, they sourced scrap iron to protect their trees.

Since then Ur Jims has regenerated about 360 hectares of wasteland with more than 2.1 million saplings.

In 2005 it began working on a 96-hectare piece of wasteland, which it named 'The Green Wall'. This piece of land has been planted with maple, plum, star anise and apple trees and raspberry bushes.

From a business that had trust as its single most important asset at its outset, Ur Jims now includes office buildings, a warehouse, a greenhouse and a fruit processing unit, as well as tractors and farm vehicles.

And – in a rarity in Mongolia – the majority of its members are still women, 32 from its total of 35.

CHRISTCHURCH, NEW ZEALAND

Te Kaihanga is the Maori word for a builder, or creator.

Between the late 1960s and the 1990s, many Maori teenagers came from New Zealand's North Island to study and work in Christchurch in its South Island.

Under a program run by New Zealand's now defunct Maori Affairs Department, these teenagers became adept in various aspects of the building trade, working together informally over the years.

In 2012, this relationship was formalised with the creation of the Te Kaihanga co-operative.

"The journey of TK Build's members underlies our future aspirations," says Barry Baker, Chairman of Te Kaihanga Cooperative. "Co-operation has existed in an informal way between the members for more than 20 years, and this provides the glue for our foundations."

It is New Zealand's first Maori trade co-operative, and it comes at a time of need for the city of Christchurch and its environs following the devastating earthquake of early 2011.

Te Kaihanga, or TK Build as it is also known, works in the residential building industry. Maori culture is known for its wood carvings in which ancient knowledge is carved into their *whares* or houses.

This page: dotCoop, Washington, USA.
Right: National Cooperative Grocers
Association (NCGA), USA.

VA
JUN   VIRGINIA   VA
09

DOTCOOP

CHAPTER 5

Supporting Co-operatives

UNITED STATES
NATIONAL COOPERATIVE GROCERS ASSOCIATION (NCGA)

When the United Nations declared 2012 the International Year of Co-operatives, the USA-based National Cooperative Grocers Association (NCGA) began celebrating with its member and associate food co-ops by shining a spotlight on their activities, and observing the unique ways they all help build a better world. NCGA's purpose is to leverage resources and offer tools for grocery co-operatives to tell their stories and deliver on their promise to provide great food and support for their local communities.

NCGA is a business services co-operative for retail food co-ops located throughout the USA. The association represents 128 food co-ops operating 165 stores in 35 states, with combined annual sales of more than USD 1.4 billion and more than 1.3 million consumer-owners. Food co-ops today enjoy greater credibility and positioning in the natural foods marketplace than ever before, and operate with increasing levels of efficiency because they have created a national organisation with continuous improvement in the food co-op sector as its mission.

The 12-year history of National Cooperative Grocers Association (NCGA) is nothing short of remarkable.

Prior to the creation of NCGA, there was no national organisation specifically serving the needs of food co-ops. In the 1980s, there was a growing awareness that food co-ops could be doing more together – communicating especially – and that strengthening connections among food co-ops was necessary work.

The Cooperative Grocers Association Midwest was founded in 1992, and was the first regional organisation to put resources towards the goal of greater collaboration. Other regions began organising in a similar fashion, and by 1996 six co-operative grocers' associations (CGAs) were operating in all corners of the country.

"We laid the groundwork by working together regionally. People participated willingly and generously. It is the enduring strength of our system," said Karen Zimbelman, NCGA's development services director.

As collaborative projects grew, the leadership of the regional CGAs believed it was imperative to have a national organisation that would be a conduit and clearinghouse for their activities. Thus in 1999, NCGA was created. Later, in 2004, the CGAs voted to dissolve their regional associations in favour of direct membership in NCGA.

At that time, not many people could have predicted that food co-op member dues would become a fraction of an operating income of more than USD 15.5 million dollars, and that NCGA would be overseeing a myriad of programs offering bottom-line savings on purchasing, marketing, store development and technical assistance. It is a testament to the members' passionate involvement that NCGA is poised to do even more in the coming decade.

One of the first and most successful programs launched nationally was a mutual buying program to take advantage of volume discounts from manufacturers. This program gave the association an economic driver, providing cost benefits to members and a marketing platform for reaching more consumers.

Robynn Shrader, NCGA's CEO, said that the reorganised NCGA allowed the food co-ops to formally consolidate their buying power, which in turn has led to tremendous member benefit. "We have seen a huge payoff. We have seen that aggregation works," said Shrader.

Now, she said, competitors continue to enter food co-op strongholds with a vengeance. This change has demanded not only a higher level of retail sophistication from co-op stores, but points to the need for growth and efficiency. The creation of NCGA's Development Cooperative subsidiary in 2008 is one way that NCGA supports the development of the sector, by assisting its members in building and adding more stores to their operations.

Food co-op membership in NCGA has proven to be invaluable for each co-op's ability to effectively compete in its own marketplace. A significant number of NCGA's member retailers have won multiple awards for retailing excellence and community leadership, in part through the programs and opportunities for professional development offered to NCGA member co-ops.

"NCGA's slogan of 'Stronger Together' epitomises the opportunities many members have discovered since joining our association," said NCGA board president Pam Mehnert. "The strength of our association is in pooling the right resources that help our members to become excellent store operators and build a stronger co-operative identity in their communities."

Given the radical changes in the economy and rapid shifts in the industry, Shrader knows it is critical that food co-operators adapt and respond by continually innovating and looking forward. As food co-ops engage with more local communities and work to build the co-operative economy, Shrader said that NCGA will continue to demonstrate even more of the value of working together. "Our focus in the future is on growth and the opportunity to bring the benefits of co-operatives to more and more communities."

SCOTLAND

SCOTTISH AGRICULTURAL ORGANISATION SOCIETY (SAOS)

The production of Scotland's 70 farmer co-operatives has increased over recent years by about 15 percent each year – 2011 saw this reach around £2.8 billion. "We're in a period of strong, sustained growth, and we expect this above-trend growth to continue for the foreseeable future," says James Graham, CEO of the Scottish Agricultural Organisation Society (SAOS). SAOS is owned by the co-operatives and provides specialist development and advice services across the farming and food industry in Scotland.

Graham continues, "It's not difficult to understand why family farmers should work together. Most farm businesses are small relative to others in their value chain. Joining forces makes perfect sense – to save costs, to secure customers and grow, to share investment and add value, to manage risks, and diversify into new opportunities. But, most importantly, we believe that farmers can help preserve their independence by co-operating to secure gains that are not available when they act individually. Co-operation is a key to sustaining vibrant rural communities that are self-reliant and enterprising."

And many of Scotland's farmers agree. Adam Marshall, a member of Borders Machinery Ring, says, "For me, it's a no-brainer really. Through the Ring, members can offer their machinery for use year-round to other members and earn more income, and they can find extra labour to help out at peak times – and all without having to go through the stress of organising it themselves. The Ring makes life much simpler and leaves us more time to get on with our farming."

Mark McCallum, his father John and son Cameron grow high quality malting barley and are members of Highland Grain. McCallum agrees that the benefits of co-operation make great sense for farmers.

"My grandfather was a founder member of one of the two groups that merged to create Highland Grain. What made sense to those guys is even more relevant in today's marketplace – working together means that we have greater power than we could ever have as individuals. I'd say the most important aspect for growers is that the co-op provides us with much more security than we'd have on our own."

Andrew Rennie is a member of Scottish Pig Producers (SPP). "For me, being part of Scottish Pig Producers provides stability and security in what can be a very volatile industry. Scottish Pig Producers has been at the forefront of developments in Scotland since it was established, and these have helped to improve quality and productivity across the whole industry. Customers of SPP know that they're assured of consistent quality, and members get a strong voice in the market, latest market information and wide-ranging economies of scale."

Co-operatives are active in most of Scotland's farming sectors, from sheep and beef production through to dairy, cereals, potatoes and vegetables, aquaculture, horticulture and timber.

"We don't have the largest co-ops, but that means we have to be smarter, more innovative and highly commercial," says James Graham.

"Agriculture must deal with huge challenges in the future. The global population is growing and food security is becoming more difficult while resources of agricultural land, water and energy are becoming scarce and very expensive.

"We have to produce more with less, and ensure that fair value is returned to farmers, so they can innovate and contribute fully. Farmers also understand that they must reduce their impact on the planet. Farmers' co-operatives operating at local, regional, national and global levels provide the responsible alternative to profit-maximising corporations."

SAOS *Family farmers – together we grow*

POLAND

NATIONAL AUDITING UNION OF WORKERS' CO-OPERATIVES (NAUWC)

First established in the 1870s, Polish workers' co-operatives constitute one of the oldest and purest forms of production co-operatives. They played a leading role in rebuilding the country in 1918, when Poland regained independence.

The National Auditing Union of Workers' Co-operatives (NAUWC) was established in Warsaw in 1991, replacing an organisation liquidated during the political transformation of Poland.

The 1990s brought policies that changed the nature of co-operatives in Poland. Auditing unions were no longer authorised to conduct business activity, which made it more difficult to provide assistance to associated co-operatives.

Acting in accordance with Polish law, NAUWC found a way to finance itself and to work with other co-operatives. Its consulting team, consisting of economists, legal advisers and certified auditors, assists co-operatives and their members on a daily basis. NAUWC established the Co-operative Assistance Fund to offer loans at low interest rates, and the Co-operative Promotion Fund to finance the publication of books and news releases on the internet, advertisements in the media and presentations for national and international fairs. It also owns the Pupils' Development Co-operative Fund.

NAUWC associates over 200 co-operatives from the manufacturing, production, service and social sectors of the economy. Its statutory activities include auditing, training and archiving documents, and are conducted through Regional Offices located in every *voivodeship* (province) in Poland.

The President and Chief Accountant Clubs, which operate in every *voivodeship*, create a valuable opportunity for members of the different co-operatives in a given region to get together, exchange experiences and co-operate with each other.

NAUWC has set up four trade agreements for fishing, metal-working, educational and medical co-operatives. NAUWC is also active at an international level. It is a member of the International Co-operative Alliance (ICA), Co-operatives Europe, the International Organisation of Industrial, Artisanal and Service Producers' Co-operatives and the European Confederation of Workers' Co-operatives, Social Co-operatives and Social and Participative Enterprises. Furthermore, NAUWC is connected with co-operatives in Denmark, Finland, Sweden, Norway, Lithuania, Estonia, the Czech Republic, Slovakia, Italy, Spain, Russia, Japan and China. It is also holding talks concerning the creation of the Polish-Chinese Co-operative Centre of Co-operation in Warsaw.

The 100 best workers' co-operatives in Poland are ranked annually by NAUWC, an event that enjoys great popularity. It also initiates a winter co-operative competition called 'Spartakiada'. NAUWC offers a wide range of training opportunities, some organised as part of the EU programs, and it supports postgraduate studies thanks to the Co-operative Development and Promotion Agency.

Every Polish *voivodeship* will be celebrating the 2012 International Year of Co-operatives. Two events will be organised at the national level: an extraordinary Management Board meeting in September combined with an 'integration' picnic, and the National Social Economy meeting in October, during which a 'Pact for the Social Economy' will be signed. NAUWC is a co-author of the Pact, whose objective is to oblige the Polish Government to act in the interests of the social economy. NAUWC has the status and authority to influence the legislative process in Poland.

NAUWC members believe that their actions confirm the statement that 'co-operatives build a better world'.

WASHINGTON, USA

Until the top-level domain name .coop was launched in January 2002, the only other options were .com, .net, .org and country-denoted domain names.

dotCoop's CEO Carolyn Hoover explains from their Washington DC base, situated in the National Cooperative Business Association's offices, how she achieved her aim of building the co-operative's business.

The Internet Corporation for Assigned Names and Numbers was lobbied to open the then exclusive list of top-level domains. In June 2011, it approved the request.

"I'm excited about how the growth in the number of domains will make people more aware of the value of what's at the end of a domain name and what it will mean to .coop," Hoover says. "In the past, people would see a .coop name and think that the .coop at the end of the domain was just a mistake. What they will come to understand is that the end of the domain means as much as the rest of the name!"

She notes that a number of .coop users have drawn attention to the .coop domain name on their websites or in emails, starting discussions about what makes a co-operative different from other businesses.

"Now people will start looking at the TLD [the last part of the domain name] and realise that .coop really means something.

"It's the way to know that you've found a business that is based on specific values and principles and not just another .com or .org," Hoover says. dotCoop will be working with the .coop registrars around the world to promote .coop to groups who want to use a domain space to identify their group or community online.

"dotCoop learned a lot of lessons after it was selected to be one of the first group of the new domains launched back in 2000. But being a part of the co-operative community has made us more, well, co-operative. We look forward to working with other new groups and sharing our 'lessons learned'."

CANADA

CANADIAN CO-OPERATIVE ASSOCIATION, CONSEIL CANADIEN DE LA COOPÉRATION ET
DE LA MUTUALITÉ, CONSEIL QUÉBÉCOIS DE LA COOPÉRATION ET DE LA MUTUALITÉ

Co-operatives touch the lives of millions of Canadians. They create jobs, revitalise communities and have a significant impact on the Canadian economy. They exist in every region of the country and virtually every economic sector – from retail, financial services and insurance; to agriculture, fishing and energy; to housing, healthcare, funeral services and social services. According to the International Co-operative Alliance, Canada has the eighth largest co-operative membership in the world.

In a country of 34 million people spread out over nearly 10 million square kilometres, networks representing co-operatives are extremely important in building and sustaining the Canadian movement. Canada has two national co-operative associations, the Canadian Co-operative Association and the Conseil canadien de la coopération et de la mutualité, which represents French-language co-operatives across Canada. Both associations are active members of ICA (International Co-operative Alliance). There are also 17 provincial associations, including the Conseil québécois de la coopération et de la mutualité, as well as credit union centrals at both the national and provincial or regional levels. Together, these networks work to promote, develop and unite co-operatives across Canada and give real meaning to the Sixth Principle – Co-operation among Co-operatives.

Québec: cradle of Canadian co-operation

While co-operatives have a long history in every province of Canada, the country's first co-operative organisations were mutual insurance companies started by Québec farmers in the 1830s. Québec, where French is the official language, is also the home of Canada's first financial services co-operative, founded by Alphonse Desjardins in 1900 and profiled elsewhere in this publication.

Today, Québec has some 3,300 co-operatives and mutuals with more than 8.8 million members, and approximately 70 percent of all Québeckers are members of at least one co-operative.

A snapshot of Canada's co-operatives:

9,000	Number of co-operatives in Canada
18 million	Total membership
155,000	People employed
100,000	Volunteer directors and committee members
$50+ billion	Annual revenue
$370+ billion	Total assets

Above: Young co-operators Erin Hancock and Marco Plourde were the MCs of the Canadian launch of the International Year of Co-operatives on 12 January 2012.

KUALA LUMPUR, MALAYSIA
ANGKASA

One of the most important principles held by ANGKASA, Malaysia's national co-operatives' organisation, is that it offers its services to members free of charge. Members pay no monthly or annual subscription fees, and there are free training courses and development programs for its membership, which includes school co-operatives. The only exception to this is a service assisting co-operatives to collect loan repayments.*

ANGKASA's wider philosophy is that the spread of co-operatives in the global economy will support the elimination of poverty and oppression and enable economic prosperity to be shared by all. It holds to the theory that co-operatives around the world have fared better in the global economic downturn than other business models.

On a regional level, ANGKASA works in co-operation with the government of Malaysia to ensure the strength of the Malaysian co-operative sector. Here it is active in Malaysia's development efforts, particularly in the areas of industry and trade, while recognising the need to work with private investors in a way that does not conflict with the co-operative sector's principles. These principles include, amongst others, putting the public interest to the fore, as well as adopting a neutral stance in politics and religion.

Promoting education is a high priority for ANGKASA. Malaysia is leading the way in co-operative education in Asia, and many schools in Asia aim to emulate Malaysia's model. People from countries including Japan, India and Fiji have visited Malaysia to learn about co-operative management studies and to participate in the School Co-operative Tourism program.

ANGKASA and its members are playing a vital role in the country's economic development.

*The Salary Deduction Service is a service that assists co-operatives to collect loan repayments. ANGKASA deducts the repayment directly from the salary of the individual and makes the payment to the co-operative, thus ensuring that there are few cases of non-repayment of loans. Only 0.6 percent of the total amount is taken as a service charge, and entities other than co-operatives that use the service are charged between one and two percent.

angkasa

CANADA

CO-OPERATIVE EDUCATION AND RESEARCH: LEADING PROGRAMS AND INTERDISCIPLINARY
RESEARCH FOCUSED ON CO-OPERATIVES

The following four Canadian education and research initiatives illustrate a spectrum of approaches to both research and education.

Interdisciplinary Graduate Program in Co-operative Studies, Centre for the Study of Co-operatives, University of Saskatchewan

Approved in 2004, the Interdisciplinary Graduate Program in Co-operative Studies offers a customised master's or doctoral program to meet the needs of future researchers, policymakers and academics. Affiliated faculty are committed to developing and offering courses that provide an understanding of co-operative theory, principles, development, structures and legislation, through their home departments of history, sociology, public policy, agricultural economics, management, economics, English and education. Thesis topics range from co-operative development to governance, policy, finance and organisational theory.

Known for its research intensiveness and emphasis on community-based research and community engagement, the Centre for the Study of Co-operatives (usaskstudies.coop) hosts the largest collection of English-language materials on co-operatives in North America. Funding partners include Credit Union Central of Saskatchewan, Federated Co-operatives Limited, Concentra Financial, The Co-operators, the Province of Saskatchewan and the University of Saskatchewan.

On Co-op Co-operative Management Certificate Program, Schulich School of Business, York University

When the Ontario Co-operative Association (known as On Co-op) discovered that the co-operative business enterprise model was rarely taught in business schools, it began to work with the Schulich School of Business (SSB) at York University. Together they created the Co-operative Management Certificate Program (http://s.coop/cmcprogram) and designed courses that provide a deep understanding of co-operative context, regulatory frameworks, governance, management, co-op development and financing.

Through the CMC Program students learn through a combination of seven online learning modules; six facilitated 'webinars' (internet seminars); and three, two-day, face-to-face intensive sessions held with SSB faculty and sector leaders.

Students in the CMC Program – now in its third year – have included co-operative and credit union managers, board members, sector leaders, and those interested in forming a co-operative business enterprise.

The six-month Co-operative Management Certificate Program is accessible and affordable and is designed to allow students to continue with their work and home lives. It is part of On Co-op's integrated lifelong co-operative learning strategy.

Research and Education Institute for Cooperatives and Mutuals of the Université de Sherbrooke / Institut de recherche et d'éducation pour les cooperatives et les mutuelles de l'université de Sherbrooke

The Research and Education Institute for Cooperatives and Mutuals of the Université de Sherbrooke / Institut de recherche et d'éducation pour les cooperatives et les mutuelles de l'université de Sherbrooke (IRECUS) was created in 1976, following a partnership between the co-operative/mutual movements in Québec and the Université de Sherbrooke.

IRECUS is committed to education, research and the dissemination of co-operative ideas.

With more than 500 graduates, the IRECUS is proud of its contribution to the development of the co-operative movement through its master's program, research activities and personalised education workshops, and through its alliances with universities and co-operative/mutual movements in Latin America and Africa.

Co-operative Management Education at Saint Mary's University

Launched in 2003, the Master of Management, Co-operatives and Credit Unions is an international management program that provides exceptional management skills to current and future co-operative leaders. The program is designed for working professionals seeking a part-time program geared to co-operatives. A Graduate Diploma in Co-operative Management is available starting in 2013 (pending final approval).

These programs are based at the Sobey School of Business, Saint Mary's University in Halifax, Nova Scotia. Students are given a deep understanding of the history and evolution of the co-operative movement. They learn strategy, leadership and people management skills, and study accounting, finance, marketing and information technology. Throughout the programs, students use their own co-operative as a case study to ensure that what they learn is relevant to their day-to-day work. These online programs draw students, faculty and researchers from around the globe and from a diversity of co-operatives and credit unions. To date, graduates and students come from eight countries, and faculty hail from Canada, USA, New Zealand and England.

To facilitate this online learning experience, strong relationships are forged during a one-week, face-to-face orientation at the start of the program and during the international study tour in the second year of the Master's program.

UNIVERSITY OF SASKATCHEWAN
Centre for the Study of Co-operatives

UNIVERSITÉ DE SHERBROOKE

SAINT MARY'S UNIVERSITY SINCE 1802
One University. One World. Yours.

WORLDWIDE

ICA COMMITTEE ON CO-OPERATIVE RESEARCH (CCR)

The International Co-operative Alliance (ICA) Committee on Co-operative Research (CCR) began its work in 1957 as the Research Officers Group. In the 1970s the group changed its name to the ICA Research, Planning and Development Group, reflecting the widening scope of its activities, and its aspirations to provide practical input to the economic and social concerns of co-operatives.

The CCR promotes and supports research activities within co-operatives and research organisations. Working at global, regional, national and local levels, the CCR's research efforts are directed towards enhancing the social and economic effectiveness of co-operatives in all sectors. In addition, the collective and cumulative work of CCR members is central to the development of co-operative studies as a field of inquiry.

Researchers meet annually at conferences organised within the ICA regions, as well as once a year at an International Conference on Co-operative Research to present their work and share ideas.

The committee consists of a diverse mix of academic disciplines and areas of expertise, which brings a multidisciplinary approach to research outcomes. Additionally, worldwide geographic perspectives provide a foundation for comparative, international and cross-cultural research. Bolstered by new research networks emerging at the regional level, coupled with greater involvement by co-operative organisations, CCR's membership is highly motivated to produce research results.

The CCR benefits from the strong commitment and leadership of the regional representatives on the executive committee and the active involvement of former CCR chairs. Support from the ICA board and staff, most visibly through the publication of the *Review of International Co-operation*, which contains articles of relevance for practitioners and academics alike, is central to the committee's continued success.

The International Year of Co-operatives presents an important opportunity for generating new research and sharing research outcomes with new audiences. The year of celebration offers the prospect of building co-operative studies into a distinct and valuable field of investigation. At the same time, the committe has a chance to increase awareness of the activities and priorities of sectoral organisations among the academic community, and, conversely, to enhance an understanding of the research community within the co-operative sector.

Working together, researchers within co-operative organisations and research institutions can generate the evidence required to demonstrate the effectiveness and potential of co-operative organisations around the world.

IRAN
IRAN CENTRAL CHAMBER OF CO-OPERATIVES (ICC)

Iran has a plan. It wants to expand its co-operative sector to account for 25 percent of GDP.

This is no small task. It would represent a five-fold lift in contribution from the co-operative sector to the national economy from the five percent of GDP it already accounts for.

At the head of this push for growth is the Iran Central Chamber of Co-operatives (ICC). Established in 1994, the chamber is the overarching national organisation responsible for all unions and co-operative companies, regardless of their size or their type of activity.

Its members are active in national as well as international economic co-operative and related organisations, operating within the framework of Iran's political and economic policies.

The Chamber of Co-operatives is active in co-operative development, with responsibility for establishing co-operatives for university graduates, as well as service, consultative and export co-operatives.

It also promotes the role of co-operatives in the nation, and to that end holds exhibitions aimed at introducing the capabilities of the co-operative sector both inside and outside of Iran.

The ICC is particularly focused on Africa where it is active in the creation of trade zones, while at home it looks for support and sponsorship of national and international co-operatives.

Paving the way for co-operative export promotions is also part of its brief, as is organising co-operation among co-ops and taking advantage of their individual potential, such as organising permanent exhibitions through regional feasibility studies. The chamber plays a part in privatisation of businesses in favour of co-operatives.

Another important role it plays is acting as a middleman in making capital, including both national and international financial resources, accessible to co-operatives.

The chamber worked co-operatively to found Iran's Cooperative Development Bank and on developing an Iranian Cooperative Fund.

The ICC is also responsible for developing an IT centre of excellence. All in all, ICC has more than 170,000 member co-operative societies with 45 million members across the nation in different economic sectors including agriculture, housing, handwoven carpets and fisheries. Its structure is based on provincial chambers in each of the 31 provinces of Iran.

Aside from its aim to grow the contribution of co-operatives to the national economy, Iran is also very concerned with the betterment of citizens' livelihoods, which co-operatives contribute to indirectly.

The chamber also plays a role in supporting workers – it offers outreach services, including training, to its member co-operatives.

As for the international context, the ICC regularly sends delegations to initiate memoranda of understanding to pave the way for further co-operation among co-operatives inside and outside Iran. As an illustration, the ICC has established a trade centre in the Kurdistan region of Iraq, which actively takes part in the Iraq market through Iranian co-operatives.

This page: Edinburgh Bicycle Co-op, Scotland and England.
Right: Capricorn Society, Australia and New Zealand.

CHAPTER 6

Battling big business

SCOTLAND; ENGLAND

"The bicycle is the noblest invention of mankind. I love the bicycle. I always have. I can think of no sincere, decent human being, male or female, young or old, saint or sinner, who can resist the bicycle."

– WILLIAM SAROYAN

This quote from the Pulitzer Prize-winning Californian novelist is proudly displayed by the Edinburgh Bicycle Co-op.

For the seven self-proclaimed 'hippies' who set up the co-operative as a bicycle repair outfit in 1977, the bike is paramount. So are the co-operative values on which the business was founded.

The co-operative model suited their politics and couldn't have worked better for their business.

Most employees of this worker co-operative become members after a year. The members – who now total 135 – believe that having ownership makes a difference to the standard of their work.

"One of the challenges of being in retail is delivering a quality experience to your customer in all aspects. In order to do this effectively, you must ensure that your customer service staff are engaged with your business," explains the co-op's Managing Director, Jeremy Miles.

"Many retailers struggle with this as they tend to pay minimum wages, provide a fairly uninteresting working environment and have a high staff turnover. As a co-operative, we are able to involve our owners in customer service. The customers are more likely to gain a positive experience from speaking to someone who has a vested interest in the co-operative."

The Edinburgh Bicycle Co-op has opened a shop in Aberdeen, and four others in England. Its flagship store in Bruntsfield, Edinburgh, has the widest selection of bicycles in Scotland.

GLASGOW, SCOTLAND

" 'I'm just finishing the ironing, then I'll get
you your dinner.' That's all I said. The next
thing I knew he had me by the throat.
So I phoned my hairdresser. It was the only
place he used to let me go by myself. She rang
Women's Aid. My hairdresser saved my life.
I was a prisoner, now it's stopped."

mediaco-op makes films that make people take notice, like the above extract from a campaign against domestic violence produced for Scottish Women's Aid. Yet its commitment to social justice hasn't been a barrier to success.

mediaco-op's animation on child abuse, *Mikey and Jools Keep Safe*, won a coveted Gold Plaque at the prestigious Chicago International Film Festival. Its BBC TV documentary *Multiple* (in which

Scottish actor/director Alison Peebles discloses her struggle with multiple sclerosis) won a gold award at the Chicago International Film Festival and a silver at the Houston International Film Festival. Its campaigning web clip *Courage*, made about refugees in Scotland in co-operation with the Scottish Refugee Council, was featured on the homepage of the United Nations Refugee Agency (UNHCR). The feature-length documentary mediaco-op co-produced, *Man for a Day*, premiered at the 2012 Berlin International Film Festival.

Like the subjects of many of its films, mediaco-op is a minority figure. In a media industry increasingly dominated by giant, commercially driven corporations, mediaco-op thrives as a small, worker-owned co-operative.

But as its awards demonstrate, being small doesn't mean compromising on quality. Purely commercial motivations are not always required to make good films.

As mediaco-op's Louise Scott says proudly, "Our commitment to excellence is driven by our passion for a better world".

KALAMAZOO, USA

The 100-mile eating concept (choosing to eat food mostly sourced within 100 miles of your home) was made famous by two Canadians who wrote stories for the internet, which won them a book deal, which landed them a television program.

The members of the People's Food Co-op of Kalamazoo, Michigan are applying this ecologically interesting concept to their business. The co-operative organises a regular '100 mile market', selling only produce grown within a 100-mile radius.

But sustainability is only part of its activities. The co-operative, which opened shop in 1970, moved into new purpose-built premises in 2011. That was the end result of changes to its structure that began in 1998. From charging an annual membership fee of USD 30, the co-operative converted to an equity-based structure. This saw its membership grow exponentially, from 450 to more than 1,650.

The People's Food Co-op is currently exploring new possibilities. "We've settled into our new store really well,"

says General Manager Chris Dilley. "Now we're starting the community conversation about where we can do more."

The co-operative's board has come up with a novel plan. To begin the dialogue about 'what's next', the board is asking members to read two books and watch a movie, and it specifies their titles.

Their choice of material gives a good idea of which direction the dialogue with members might take. One of the books, *Seed Folks*, is a novel for teenagers based around a community garden in a city.

BERLIN, GERMANY

"Nobody gives us a chance – but we'll grab it with both hands."

SO READ THE FIRST EDITION OF THE BERLIN DAILY NEWSPAPER *TAZ* IN 1979

The newspaper adopted a co-operative structure 12 years later. Fast forward to 2012 and the paper is still the only publication in Germany owned by its readers.

In a dramatically shifting media landscape, *Taz*'s co-operative structure ensures the independence of its journalism. Daily mastheads are under increasing pressure to replace dwindling advertising revenues and to compete with the rising forces of the internet. These pressures have had a myriad of effects on the quality of daily journalism around the globe. The evils of self-censorship have eroded the independence of journalists in all corners of the world, largely through fear of job loss. This,

combined with business imperatives dominating editorial decision-making, has steadily eroded reportage once written without fear or favour.

The *Taz* Co-operative has been able to rise above the travails that plague other newspapers. Owned by about 11,000 readers, it has a solid capital base of about €11 million and about 250 contributors.

Thirty-three years after its formation, the *Taz* remains independent and the same deep-seated beliefs guide the publication.

"We can't let up on our fight to reveal the truth," declares *Taz* Editor-in-Chief Ines Pohl.

Above left: Photography Jonas Maron

LEICESTER, ENGLAND

In 1989, Great Britain was still recovering from the global stock market crash of 1987. In Highfields Parish in Leicester, discussion about the problems faced by the city's financially disadvantaged led to talk of establishing a credit union.

The strategy was suggested by the new parish priest, Father John Lally. He originally hailed from County Mayo, Ireland, where the credit union movement was an integral part of the community. Father John gathered the 24 signatures necessary to form a credit union. He recalls that many people didn't know what they were signing for, but did so regardless.

The Registry for Friendly Societies advised Father John that the credit union must be based on a common bond, and that in this case that bond could be the mile-and-a-half square area around the church. A common bond is a substitute for collateral in the early stages of a financial institution.

Ultimately that plan was abandoned in favour of all the local churches – Catholic, Anglican, Methodist and Moravian – coming together to form Highfields Churches Together, thereby providing the backing needed to launch the credit union.

Clockwise was established in January 1992. It celebrated its 20-year anniversary in 2012, in the UN International Year of Co-operatives.

SWEDEN; NORWAY

"Men in black plundering estates" was how newspapers depicted the Swedish funeral industry and its monopoly in 1944. So outrageous was the price of burying your dead that the debate reached as far as the Swedish Parliament.

Moving into action, the Church of Sweden approached the Swedish Cooperative Union, the KF, for help. And help it did, establishing Stockholm's Funeral Association in 1945 to promote ethical practices in the funeral industry.

A year later Stockholm's Funeral Association had opened its first office, followed closely by agencies in Malmö, Göteborg, Eskilstuna and Västerås. The idea of a co-operative funeral agency spread, and soon associations were established over the country.

Little more than a decade later, in 1958, the Funeral Agencies confederation was founded. Both the association and its confederation were supported financially and organisationally by the KF.

In 1970 the association was re-named Fonus, from *funus*, the Latin word for funeral. The association began to operate on its own,

with less assistance from the KF. Larger, regional associations were formed and operations were centralised.

As well as taking increasing control of its own operation, Fonus began to look strategically at growth. In order to give member associations more control over pricing and delivery of coffins, the subsidiary Fonus Träindustri was established. Soon afterwards this subsidiary started to manufacture coffins.

By 1994, Fonus had set up in Norway where there are today 20 T.S. Jacobsen and Fonus offices. In the past it has also had offices in Finland and Denmark.

"Since the end of the forties we have been recognising the delicate nature of family law, meeting our customers' needs throughout their life," said Mats Liste, CEO at Fonus. "Today our legal agency – Sweden's largest family law agency and an important partner to Fonus – has 34 establishments around the country."

AUSTRALIA; NEW ZEALAND

CAPRICORN SOCIETY

For a small, unofficial auto parts buying group which, in the early 1970s, had little understanding of co-operatives, Capricorn Society's founders were nonetheless big on co-operative values.

The company was formed by a group of Western Australian service station owners hoping to level out the competitive playing field between themselves and 'big' business.

"Getting suppliers was the breakthrough we had always needed," says founding member Brian Tulloch. "The suppliers could see that they would not have any bad debts because the co-operative carried all of the risk and guaranteed payments of the account. Besides this, they increased sales volume to such an extent that they could afford to give us a better price."

With interest growing from other potential members, the buying group registered as a co-operative. They decided it was a form of enterprise well suited to small business operators in the retail motor industry and less complex than other business models. Their aim was not to make a profit for the co-operative itself, or to provide capital gains for outside investors, but to maximise the efficiency, economy and profitability of each member's own enterprise.

Current CEO Greg Wall says, "The co-operative model was an ideal form through which groups of people could be helped to cope more effectively with the economic and social challenges that affected businesses at the time."

The name Capricorn was chosen because its Western Australian founders "wanted to stretch around the world like that invisible line called the Tropic of Capricorn". That ambition began to be realised. In 1988 the society expanded into New South Wales, and three years later it was operating in every Australian state. It then opened up its membership to the auto paint and panelbeating industry, and to motor trade businesses in New Zealand.

Russell Green, the owner of an Auckland automotive repair workshop, was one of the first New Zealanders to join. His fellow New Zealanders, he says, "are very aware of how co-operatives run and operate, due to their involvement with them in the dairy industry. So the co-operative principles and philosophies were readily accepted and appreciated."

Capricorn, now a corporatised trading co-operative, has a growing membership base of more than 14,000 international members and works with more than 2,200 suppliers.

"The true success of any co-operative," says Wall, "lies in the hearts and minds of its members. We work closely with them, drawing on local experience, which plays an important role in the development of member and supplier relationships and the power of the co-operative."

Russell Becker runs an automotive repair workshop in northwest Sydney and joined up in the early 1990s, since his various parts suppliers "all end up on the one Capricorn invoice, and you also get a better buy price because you're part of a larger group". He has incorporated the philosophy of co-operation in his company, but says that many small business owners in the mechanics trade remain cynical about the concept.

"They go 'Is there a funny handshake that goes with that?' It's just a case that even though my small business and the one down the road are in competition, if you work together you can both become more profitable and more efficient."

CHAPTER 7

Having a positive influence

Left: The Big Carrot, Canada.
This page: A detail from the Rumala Sahib (ornamental prayerbook cover) at the Canadian Ramgarhia Society's gurdwara (Sikh house of worship) in Surrey, BC. Vancity provided the Society with a loan to repay the congregation for its financing of the gurdwara's construction.

FRANCE; QUÉBEC, ONTARIO, CANADA

The CUMA (Coopérative d'Utilisation de Matériel Agricole or "co-operative for the use of farm implements") emerged from French farmers' need to mechanise after World War II.

Through CUMAs, farmers own and operate farm agricultural machinery collectively, making it both more affordable and more efficiently utilised. The main activity of these co-operatives is harvesting but some are also active in irrigation, forestry and drainage. Due to the technological evolution of agriculture, CUMA projects have recently become even more diversified. There is a big boom in small-scale food-processing, and a growing number of these plants are now run by CUMAs.

In rural areas, an increasing number of jobs are carried out by local CUMA partners. Many schools, for example, are using wood pellets supplied by a CUMA to power boiler heaters. In some rural communities CUMAs function even more efficiently by renting out their machinery to local authorities to complete a range of works, including snow clearing in winter.

While farmers make up only five percent of the workforce in France, they occupy about two-thirds of its territory. In areas such as the Lozère in France's deep southwest, the local CUMA has developed to become the leading economic force.

By 1997 France's national federation of CUMAs identified more than 13,000 of these machinery co-operatives, and they could also be found in the French-speaking Canadian province of Québec and neighbouring Ontario.

HORSENS, DENMARK

The pork industry has become big business in Denmark.

The 125-year-old organisation Danish Crown, which originated in the co-operative slaughterhouses of Horsens in central Denmark, is central to the national industry's success. Today it is a limited company owned by the co-operative society Leverandørselskabet Danish Crown Amba.

By the 1930s Danish Crown was awash with orders for its bacon from the United Kingdom. The company's success as an exporter meant it couldn't keep up with Britain's demand for Danish bacon.

Now, 80 years on, Danish Crown is experiencing the same kind of insatiable desire for its pork products from China. It is one of the few businesses outside China that is allowed to directly export its products into the country. Danish Crown's state-of-the-art slaughterhouses in Horsens, the most modern in the world, struggle to meet Chinese demand.

Chinese and Europeans tend to eat different cuts of pork, and this has helped to make Danish Crown the world's biggest pork exporter.

CALGARY, CANADA

CALGARY CO-OPERATIVE ASSOCIATION LTD (CALGARY CO-OP)

Everyone is welcome to shop at Calgary Co-op. Your one-dollar, one-time investment makes you a member and an owner, and buys a lifetime of benefits.

Locally owned, locally operated, Calgary Co-operative Association Ltd (Calgary Co-op) is one of the largest co-operatives in North America, with over 3,300 employees and over 440,000 members.

Calgary Co-op opened its first food store in 1956, with a membership of 1,000. Over the years, the co-operative has been committed to providing its members with quality products and exceptional service, and contributing to its community. Thanks to this commitment Calgary Co-op has been able to open 24 food stores within and around Calgary. It also runs 28 gas bars, seven travel offices, two home healthcare centres and 22 wines and spirits locations, including one in Edmonton, a new location for the co-operative.

The one-dollar lifetime membership of Calgary Co-op includes many unique privileges. Each year, profits are shared with its members in the form of an annual member refund. The member refund for 2011 was CAD 30 million, and since 1956 a total of CAD 639 million has been paid out in cash and share equity. Members receive three cents per litre in grocery saving coupons every time they purchase fuel at one of its gas bars, 25 of which offer full serve. Its pharmacy delivers prescriptions free of charge, and in-store clinics offer flu shots and advice on managing heart disease, osteoporosis and diabetes.

Its Bags to Riches program encourages members to care for the environment by reusing grocery bags. For each reused bag, three cents may be credited to the member's purchase or to designated charities that are selected by Calgary Co-op employees.

As a locally owned and operated co-operative, Calgary Co-op believes in supporting local producers. Many of its products are exclusively sourced from Calgary and Alberta, and all of its fresh pork, beef and poultry are from western Canada.

In an effort to meet the needs of its members, Calgary Co-op has been expanding its selection, introducing organic, gluten-free and ethnic products. It continues to adapt and to offer its members the quality products and service they have come to expect, all at competitive prices.

Calgary Co-op is proud to take a leadership role in supporting the community. In 2011, it donated more than CAD 3.5 million dollars to local not-for-profits and charitable organisations including Meals on Wheels, the Food Bank and the YWCA.

To celebrate the 2012 UN Year of Co-operatives, Calgary Co-op, jointly with the First Calgary Financial bank, made a five-year donation to support an affordable housing initiative undertaken by The Mustard Seed (an organisation working with poor and homeless people). This community investment reflects Calgary Co-op's co-operative values in a unique and meaningful way. Calgary Co-op truly believes its members come first and works towards making every shopping experience memorable.

CHAPECÓ, BRAZIL

What do beef, poultry, pork, dairy and pizza have in common? In the Brazilian city of Chapecó, the production and sale of these products sustains lives.

Dairy and pizza are just two of the 700 products offered by one of Brazil's most successful co-operatives, Co-opercentral Aurora, whose membership includes more than 60,000 farmers.

Co-opercentral Aurora has had a fundamental impact on rural communities and the economy by supplying electricity to the countryside.

It also provides housing, sanitation and technical assistance to rural families. Small farmers formed eight regional agricultural co-operatives in 1969. This act of co-operation enabled them to industrialise production.

Co-opercentral Aurora's headquarters has grown into large scale agro-industrial facilities, including 10 sales departments, four animal feed manufacturers and three grain storage units, as well as enormous chicken and pig farming operations.

The customers have followed. Co-opercentral Aurora has more than 100,000 business customers, 31 distributors and 15,000 workers.

Aurora also acts as an educator, ensuring its small farmer members can benefit from advances in agricultural research. Thanks to Aurora's economic protection, farmers have much better access to up-to-date technology and agricultural techniques, allowing them to diversify production.

SLOVAKIA

Gold without wisdom is but clay.

– TRADITIONAL SLOVAK SAYING

This saying could apply to Coop Jednota, Slovakia's largest domestic retail chain, which undertakes to sell only products that are not harmful to human health.

Through the control and oversight of its member base, Coop Jednota has been able to expand through the 2002 merger of Coop Centrum with the Slovak Union of Consumer Co-operatives. Meanwhile, it has increased its share of the national market to 20 percent by establishing a retail presence in virtually every village, town and city in the nation.

Above all, Jednota's co-operative structure guarantees the integrity of its assets by ensuring they cannot be misappropriated.

Coop Jednota is an impressive reflection of Slovakia's proud co-operative tradition. The country was home to the first credit co-operative and farmer's co-operative in mainland Europe. Gazdovský spolok ('Farmer's Association') was founded in 1845.

COOP Jednota has continued to make its mark in European co-operative history. In 2010 it won an international award for the integration of its commercial, economic and educational activities – including its customer loyalty scheme, sales evaluation analysis and electronic contracts register – into a single web portal.

The portal won the European IT Excellence Award 2010 for the European Independent Software Vendors – Enterprise Application category. It can be accessed by anyone, from suppliers of products to consumer co-operatives.

UNITED KINGDOM
THE CO-OPERATIVE GROUP

In 2013, The Co-operative Group, based in Manchester in the northwest of England, will celebrate its 150th birthday. The northwest of England is where the modern consumer co-operative movement began, and the anniversary will be a moment of great pride for its members. The celebrations will be an opportunity for The Group to reflect on the contribution it has made to co-operation in the United Kingdom and overseas, and to consider what it might offer in the future.

Previously known as the Co-operative Wholesale Society, it had become a powerhouse of co-operative manufacturing by the start of the 20th century, supplying co-operative branded goods, from bootlaces to biscuits, to more than a thousand local co-operative societies. It also supplied co-operatives in locations as far afield as New York and the African Gold Coast. Its address – 1 Balloon Street, Manchester – became almost as well known internationally as 10 Downing Street and Buckingham Palace.

In 1872 it opened its Loan and Deposit Department, the forerunner of The Co-operative Bank, and in 1896 it purchased its first farm at Roden in Shropshire. Today, The Group is the United Kingdom's largest commercial farmer. Through numerous mergers and acquisitions, The Group now controls over 80 percent of co-operative trade in the United Kingdom and is one of the largest consumer co-operatives in the world. The Group comprises seven million individual members.

Food, financial services (banking and insurance), pharmacies, funeral arrangements, legal services, life-planning, motor vehicles and electrical goods constitute its core businesses. It also runs security and clothing businesses and has established a joint venture with Thomas Cook, the United Kingdom's largest travel agency.

The Group's turnover last year was 13.3 billion pounds. It employs more than 102,000 people, and runs more than 5,000 outlets that serve more than 21 million customers a week.

Its Estates Department manages more than 10,000 properties and has recently announced a joint venture to re-develop the 20-acre complex of buildings it owns in central Manchester to create a vibrant new quarter for the city. Its new purpose-built office in Angel Square in Manchester is one of the most environmentally sustainable office buildings in Europe, demonstrating The Group's ethical standards, as well as its financial strength and belief in its long-term future.

The Group is recognised in the United Kingdom as the most ethical retailer and financial services provider on the high street. Its policy on banking ethics has just marked its 20th anniversary. It pioneered fair trade in the United Kingdom and has been recognised with industry awards for its leadership role in animal welfare and in addressing climate change. Informed by its members' priorities, The Group's social goals are to protect the environment, keep local communities thriving, tackle global poverty, inspire young people and invest in the future of co-operation. It has developed a program linked to its business planning, which aims to deliver on these priorities. Its long-term business strategy is to expand its two biggest businesses, food and banking, and maintain a 'challenger' brand in the other sectors in which it operates. Len Wardle, Chair of The Group, believes that the co-operative model has yet to realise its full potential in the United Kingdom.

"We are currently developing a marketing strategy that will link up all of our family of businesses and demonstrate our trustworthiness and the commercial responsibility that comes with the co-operative model of business ownership," he says.

The **co-operative**

SEOUL, SOUTH KOREA

NATIONAL AGRICULTURAL COOPERATIVE FEDERATION (NACF)

Half a century ago Korea was one of the poorest countries in the world. The GDP per capita was lower than that of the least developed countries in any continent. In 1961, the National Agricultural Co-operative Federation (NACF) was established to help eradicate poverty and to improve the socio-economic status of the farming community. Since then NACF has played a crucial role in the development of the Korean economy, and the modernisation of agriculture and rural communities.

Today, now established as a modern cultural and economic power, Korea is a prominent member of the G20 group of nations. Many young people in Asia and all over the world follow the so-called 'Korean wave' of Korean pop culture – TV dramas and K-pop music.

In the same way, the NACF has grown to be a successful co-operative that hundreds of professionals from agricultural businesses around the world look to every year. According to the International Co-operative Alliance's 2011 Global 300 project, the NACF was ranked as the ninth largest co-operative and the second largest agricultural co-operative in the world.

NACF is a multi-purpose co-operative, which manages four main business divisions: agricultural marketing and supply, livestock marketing and supply, banking and insurance, and an 'extension' (guidance) service. As of July 2012, the NACF serves its members and customers through 27 subsidiaries and two affiliate organisations. It represents 2.44 million individual members – more than 80 percent of all Korean farmers.

Agricultural marketing and supply is the most essential service offered by the NACF because it directly involves ensuring higher returns and benefits to member farmers. It includes agricultural marketing in both production and consumption areas, and grain and farm supply. More than half of the products used in Korean agriculture are provided through NACF and its member co-operatives. They also supply two percent of agricultural products sold to consumers.

NACF's livestock marketing and supply business promotes resilience and sustainable growth in the livestock industry in Korea. It focuses on the international competitiveness of domestic livestock producers by improving breeding stock, reducing the input costs of livestock farming and supporting distribution.

Its banking business (NH Bank) serves 19.3 million customers with 43.9 million bank accounts, while member co-operatives provide banking services to 27.7 million customers with 77.8 million bank accounts. Taking into account its 36.7 million overlapping customers, approximately 70 percent of the national population is currently using the NH Bank or its member co-operatives. This extensive client base is derived from its diverse banking services including private banking, retail banking, corporate banking, insurance, credit card, mutual credit and, most of all, its convenient nationwide branches.

Its 'extension' service conducts various activities representing farmers' interests and rights, and supporting the welfare and cultural activities of the farming community to achieve a better quality of life.

It also engages in research and development of new technologies in the field. Its exchange programs between urban and rural communities contribute to the balanced development of the national economy.

In March 2012, the NACF established the NongHyup Agribusiness Group and NongHyup Financial Group with the aim of supporting sustainable growth through greater efficiency and specialisation. The internal and external business environment for the Korean agricultural sector has been gradually worsening.

Foreign Trade Agreements between Korea and other major economies, such as the USA, the European Union and China, have been implemented or are under negotiation, and these threaten the economic survival of Korean farmers. In addition, farmer numbers are decreasing, and farmers' groups are at a disadvantage when negotiating prices with powerful new supermarket giants.

Co-operation with its member co-operatives, subsidiaries and holding companies has been of critical importance for NACF during the period of transition since the new business ventures were undertaken.

A global co-operative for mutual growth is the NACF's vision for the future, founded on core values such as ethical management, co-operation for mutual growth, creative innovation, environmental sustainability and social responsibility.

NATIONAL AGRICULTURAL
COOPERATIVE FEDERATION

CANADA
THE CO-OPERATORS

In 1945, a group of prairie farmers who had lost most of their belongings, their savings and their life insurance during the Great Depression had a dream. Disillusioned with conventional insurance practices, they were determined to build a new co-operative insurance company that would put people before profits. Little did they know their voluntary actions would become a cornerstone of the Canadian co-operative movement.

Many obstacles confronted them – inexperience with the insurance business, few assets, tough competition and a sparsely populated country with people scattered across miles of prairies, farmland, coastal regions and mountain valleys.

Undaunted, they rolled up their sleeves and persevered to build what is now one of Canada's leading multi-product insurance and financial services organisations.

Bill Belliveau began his career with The Co-operators in 1949. Recently married, he didn't want to begin his married life in debt by buying a car, but he was determined to be able to get around town to sell insurance.

Bill turned to the most reliable mode of transportation he could afford – a bicycle. He rode his bicycle for several months, selling his first policy in March 1950, before he traded it in for a 1937 Oldsmobile worth CAD 475.

Bill's trademark bicycling to wherever his business took him was later depicted in a television commercial for The Co-operators.

Insurance agent Pat Powell, eager to serve his clients on their terms and build his business, realised that he had to be innovative in managing his client relationships. With no office in Stratford, Ontario, Pat worked from home and spent a great deal of time driving on back roads to meet with local farmers, his largest client base.

More often than not he found potential clients out in the fields, so he would go to them, often conducting his business seated on large tractor tyres or bales of hay. Eventually, Pat purchased a Volkswagen van, converting it into an 'office-on-wheels'.

Equipped with a propane heater and all of his manuals, and painted with the words 'R.W. Pat Powell Mobile Office', Pat's van met with his clients wherever they were. The decked-out VW van, shown in television commercials in 2006, was a local landmark from 1958 until 1961.

Keleigh Annau from Vancouver, BC founded Lights Out Canada, an annual event when Canadian schools turn off their lights and study climate change. She was an ideal candidate to attend The Co-operators first IMPACT! Youth Conference for Sustainability Leadership in 2009.

That first conference brought 180 Canadian university and college students inspired by the idea of sustainability together with academic, government and industry leaders. They developed practical solutions and practices intended to bring about lasting changes. It was also an important opportunity to introduce participants to the co-operative movement, and for them to learn about the co-operative business model from leaders and mentors.

To continue supporting IMPACT! alumni's sustainability ideas and solutions, The Co-operators Foundation IMPACT! Fund was created in 2009. Annau, who returned to IMPACT! 2011 as an alumni facilitator, has received three grants totalling CAD 17,000 to further the work of Lights Out Canada. The funding has enabled Annau to reach out to students across the country by recruiting and supporting provincial ambassadors. It also paid for graphic design and translation of the Lights Out Canada curriculum into French.

It's just two foundational co-operative principles – putting people before profit and investing in the community – that have become embedded into The Co-operators values. Today, with more than a million clients nationwide, it remains true to those roots and to the progressive vision of a small group of prairie farmers in 1945.

BRITISH COLUMBIA, CANADA
VANCITY

All financial institutions are community assets, and how they invest and operate affects a community's wellbeing. Vancity, Canada's largest credit union, based in the western province of British Columbia, takes this responsibility seriously.

Whereas many financial institutions focus on short-term profits for the benefit of shareholders, Vancity's work is founded on the principle that wealth includes more than just financial wellbeing, and means meeting the long-term needs of people and communities.

Vancity's goal is to create a positive impact through all its operations – from how it makes money to how its money is spent and invested. Its values-based banking model is grounded in the local economy and the belief that people only truly prosper when they're connected to a vibrant, healthy community.

The credit union has developed a sustainable business strategy, based on offering financial advice and competitive products and services, to help build the wealth of its nearly half a million members. Members' deposits are invested in and loaned to local businesses and organisations that create a positive economic, social and environmental impact in the community. Some beneficial results have been job creation and support, reduction of greenhouse gas emissions and increased home ownership.

Following are some examples of Vancity's impact lending:

- Vancity member A Bread Affair is British Columbia's only certified-organic artisan bakery and the only one in the Greater Vancouver area that bakes '100-mile' bread. Vancity financed the bakery's expansion and promoted A Bread Affair through various marketing initiatives. As a result of Vancity's support, A Bread Affair has doubled its capacity and continues to support local farmers.

- In 2013, the Songhees Wellness Centre will open its doors as a community gathering place, amalgamating the First Nation government's administration, education and health services. Previously, the First Nation operated in mobile offices and had no cultural centre or centre for elderly or young people. Vancity

financed a construction loan for the Wellness Centre by treating the First Nation as a local government and securing the loan with projected future lease and tax revenues. The Wellness Centre, a 'green' building that has received Leadership in Energy and Environmental Design (LEED) certification, will also provide a community centre, sports facility and a convention centre, and will be a tourist destination for Victoria, British Columbia.

- The Richmond Society for Community Living offers programs and services for individuals with developmental disabilities and their families. For more than 10 years Vancity has supported the Society with preferred rates, grants, investments, access, financial services and advice for the society and its clients.

In addition to impact lending, each year Vancity shares its profits with its members and the community, providing support for initiatives like local organic food production, affordable housing and financial literacy.

Between 1994 and 2012, Vancity distributed more than CAD 221.2 million through its Shared Success program.

In May 2011 Vancity became certified as a Living Wage Employer – the largest organisation in Canada to do so – because of its commitment to providing its employees with a wage that meets the needs of daily living and provides some discretionary income.

Vancity invests in local businesses that produce green products and services, finances green buildings and helps to build capacity within the community.

It seeks to minimise any negative environmental or social impact and reduce reputational and credit risk by carefully choosing its suppliers. It has an 'Ethical Policy' that is used as the framework for deciding which organisations to do business with. The policy covers ethical business practices, environmental leadership, respect and fair treatment, and healthy and peaceful communities. It is applied to relationships with business and not-for-profit members, suppliers, treasury relationships, strategic partners and grant recipients.

Vancity is a member of the Global Alliance for Banking on Values, an independent global network of values-based financial institutions. The Alliance aims to deliver on a lofty goal – to touch the lives of a billion people with sustainable banking by 2020. It seeks to deal in 'good money', which doesn't make any trade-offs between what people want – products, service, advice and price, or what people need – long-term social, environmental and economic sustainability. Their promise to members and their communities is simple: 'We make good money by putting money to good.'

Opposite page: With financing from Vancity, certified-organic bakery A Bread Affair doubled its capacity and increased its support for local agriculture and farmers. Top left: A woman facing the Rumala Sahib at the Canadian Ramgarhia Society's gurdwara (Sikh house of worship) in Surrey, BC, where thousands of free meals are served weekly to people of every race and religion. Using a non-traditional loan model, Vancity provided the Society with a loan to repay the congregation for its financing of the gurdwara's construction. Top right: Carver Butch Dick Jr., putting the finishing touches on a welcome post for the Songhees Wellness Centre, which Vancity financed.

SANTO ANDRÉ, BRAZIL

In the 1960s the people of the city of Santo André in Brazil's South east had to travel to the state capital, São Paulo, to shop at a supermarket. A group of employees of the giant French chemical company Rhodia decided to take the matter into their own hands. They founded a retail co-operative.

Cooperhodia Consumer Co-operative was formed in October 1954, and news of it spread quickly through the ranks of Rhodia's staff. Soon the initiative was known to all the company's employees, and the co-operative grew. Its first warehouse became a self-service store, replacing the original counter service system. It was the first self-service store in the region. By 1973 Cooperhodia had grown to comprise five working units.

Later, due to the expansion of supermarket chains in the metropolitan region of São Paulo, the co-operative's board of directors decided to alter its statutes and extend its business beyond Rhodia staff. In 1976, the co-operative threw open its doors to the public for the first time.

As its business broadened, it simplified its name to Coop – Consumer Co-operative. Each of these changes benefited the co-operative, resulting in more members and more stores.

Coop's main products these days are consumer and durable goods. Its original brands are still part of the range of products. Coop Plus, for example, distributes around 500 goods in 100 categories.

"We seek to promote cultural and wellbeing programs, as well as help the community. In 2010, we donated over 150 tonnes of goods to charitable organisations. Coop is an enterprise worried about social issues," says its President, José Antonio Monte.

Coop can afford to be charitable. In 2010 its turnover was around R$ 1.5 billion, and it registered a surplus of R$ 8.4 billon, distributed proportionately among its members. This earned it 13th place in the ranking of Brazilian supermarkets, according to the industry's national association.

MALAYSIA

A bank whose operations are as wide-ranging as those of Bank Rakyat can afford to change the way it does business.

In 2003, 49 years after its foundation, Malaysia's Bank Rakyat, one of Asia's largest co-operative banks, embraced an operating system based on Shariah (Islamic legal) principles.

Since then, Bank Rakyat has been able to further extend its operations to the Malaysian islands of Sabah and Sarawak.

Bank Rakyat is driven by its commitment to provide affordable financial facilities to support agriculture, fishing, housing, transportation and business, and to encourage saving and thrift among its members.

It also initiated the Rakan Koop program, which helps small- and medium-sized co-operatives upgrade and improve their management skills, as well as providing training and advice on diversifying their businesses.

And, of course, Rakan Koop provides advisory services in the Shariah-based financing system it has embraced.

TRENTINO, ITALY

Wine trellises fill the fertile valley floor of the Rotaliana Plain, where the municipality of Mezzocorona is often described as 'the most beautiful wine garden of Europe'.

In this region of Trentino, northern Italy, rich with Roman ruins and medieval buildings, the headquarters of the Mezzacorona co-operative is striking for its modernity. The co-operative is housed in a steel-enmeshed three-storey office block with a low-lying grass-roofed building.

What began with 20 grape-grower members has expanded to include 1,600 growers. Demonstrating the dominance of the co-operative model in the region, Mezzacorona has become the single largest producer of Pinot Grigio and Chardonnay in Italy.

"The value added by Mezzacorona is €40 million," says Fabio Rizzoli, the co-operative's CEO. "It's a lot of wealth, but it is well distributed. We do not disdain profit; it is one of our principal objectives. However, it is not the only one. I was born in the country and I know that when you plant a vine you have to take care of it and

wait at least five to six years before seeing results. Long-term projects are ultimately the most ethical, and they yield lasting and satisfactory results for all stakeholders.

"Today's managers are very aggressive and want to see results immediately, but this is not sustainable and creates imbalances like the ones we've seen provoke the financial crisis," he says.

In wine production terms, Mezzacorona is big business. It mass-produces wine for global markets. "To run a business, it takes balance and attention to the needs of all stakeholders," explains Rizzoli. "I have always aimed to reconcile the interests of the company with those of the worker, the community, the environment, the consumer and the producer, and never engaged in rampant profit-seeking."

Today, the traditional pergola methods of growing vines have been intertwined with the modern espaliered method, which enables mechanised production at Mezzacorona.

The co-operative's production, like its architecture and its business, is a mixture of old and new.

BOGOTÁ, COLOMBIA

There are many measures of success. In Latin America owning your own football team has to be one of them – especially when that football team wins the national league.

By this measure, and by a number of others, La Equidad Seguros is a success. With assets of USD 135 million it is one of the largest insurers in Colombia. And it has become so by providing insurance products custom-designed for Colombia's most needy.

La Equidad arose from a 1968 study group led by two men who, at different times, headed the global co-operative insurance body International Cooperative and Mutual Insurance Federation (ICMIF). Raymond Lemaire was then head of one of the world's largest co-operative insurers, P&V, while Klas Bach went on to become CEO of the giant Swedish co-operative insurer, Folksam. Through their efforts La Equidad was established in 1970.

Research showed that many Colombians were interested in buying insurance, but existing products did not cater to their needs. La Equidad responded by developing products that were highly successful.

One of its greatest successes was a micro-insurance product developed with funding from the USA aid agency United States Agency for International Development (USAID).

After more than four decades in business, La Equidad is now owned by more than 1.5 million Colombians.

SINGAPORE
NTUC FAIRPRICE CO-OPERATIVE LTD

When NTUC FairPrice Co-operative Ltd was founded in 1973, it committed itself to addressing the rising cost of living. A global oil crisis had triggered rising food prices. As prices shot up, the co-operative helped to stabilise them, setting benchmark prices and preventing profiteering.

Through subsequent years, especially during periods of economic downturn and recession, FairPrice remained vigilant on prices, absorbed consumer taxes and on several occasions was the first to drop prices of essentials to help cushion rising food costs that would inevitably impact lower wage earners.

From one supermarket, FairPrice has grown to become Singapore's largest retailer, with a network of more than 100 outlets in various retail formats. It has kept pace with the changing needs of its customers, while remaining committed to its social mission and aspiring to be Singapore's leading retailer with a heart. This large and successful co-operative is, in fact, a part of Singapore's National Trade Union Congress (NTUC).

As a social enterprise, FairPrice's business model is different from other businesses, which strive mainly to increase their bottom line. FairPrice is also committed to its social mission of moderating the cost of living, benefiting its members and the community. At FairPrice, doing well means doing good.

Gerry Lee, Managing Director (business groups) at FairPrice, is one of the co-operative's longest-serving staff members. He has seen first-hand how FairPrice has continued to serve the community by moderating the cost of living.

"Its measures included importing rice direct from Thailand and selling it affordably to consumers in Singapore amidst fluctuating food prices during the 1970s oil crisis to curb profiteering," Lee says. "In the 1980s, FairPrice house-brand products were launched to provide affordable daily essentials, and in the 1990s the EDLP (Every Day Low Pricing) program was introduced to offer a value basket of popular essential items. During the SARS and Bird Flu periods in the mid 2000s, we ensured that vegetable prices and eggs remained stable and curbed profiteering."

Lee recalls how difficult it was for the co-operative and its staff during this period.

"We were all afraid of contracting this new unknown disease but we knew we had to continue doing our jobs. The media continued to report on an increasing number of people falling sick, but our customers still needed their groceries. We were not going to let them down and kept prices stable. We also had to assure our customers that the food we were providing was safe and that they need not panic buy and overstock food.

"Unfortunately, some of our staff got sick as well and we had to immediately quarantine them. It was a very trying and emotional time for them and their families. To this day, I still remember how afraid and sad it was for all of us."

After a lifetime of service, Lee recollects how he first got involved in one of Singapore's most successful co-operatives.

"Back then, I was young and looking for a job to feed myself. Little did I know that the supermarket I was working for stood for so much more. Now, after 35 years, having seen all the good that FairPrice has done for the community and what co-operatives really stand for, my decision to join was one of the best I've ever made."

Gerry Lee started as a supervisor at a FairPrice store in the 1970s and he went on to manage several. In the early 1980s, he moved to the purchasing department where he headed the rice and sugar division, and then became General Manager of the purchasing division. In the late 2000s he returned to supermarket operations and became FairPrice's General Manager before assuming his current position of Managing Director (business groups).

IRAN

THE CENTRAL UNION OF RURAL AND AGRICULTURAL COOPERATIVES (CURACI)

There are few countries in the world where co-operation holds a more significant position in the national economy than in Iran.

The peak organisation for rural and agricultural co-operatives, Curaci (the Central Union of Rural and Agricultural Cooperatives), has five million family members, 31 provincial level unions, 240 city level co-operatives and 9,577 stores. It is the biggest organisation in Iran across the private sector, the government sector and the co-operative sector.

To understand the importance of co-operatives in Iran, it is necessary to appreciate that co-operation has a meaningful place in the Muslim scripture, the Koran. In the Koran humans are recommended to co-operate for the good of humanity. At an organisational level that is interpreted as a business that properly satisfies human needs and results in justice and progress in society.

Curaci, which was established in 1978, acts primarily as a marketing body for its members. It markets farm crops including onions, tomatoes, pulses, corns, barley and cotton. It also takes on the marketing of garden crops such as apples, oranges, lemons, pomegranates, apricots, grapes, pistachio, walnuts and almonds.

The co-operative takes responsibility for both the local and international marketing of agricultural crops, and offers interest-free loans to its members so that they have capital to, for example, expand their activities.

Curaci operates according to government-established goals of decentralisation, self-sufficiency, competitiveness and meeting the common needs of its members. Part of this involves investing in infrastructure in order to enable production increases, therefore having a positive impact on the socio-economic status of Iranians.

TROCA
Central union of Rural & agricultural
Cooperatives of IRAN
www.trocairan.com
tel:009821-88989546
fax:009821-88964166
Email:trade@trocairan.com

curaci

LISBON, PORTUGAL

Crédito Agrícola is one of the few private Portuguese financial institutions that can claim to be funded exclusively by national capital.

The Portuguese public has been greatly pleased by the contribution this 'bank' has made to the economic and social development of many regions of the country. It has generated benefits for the communities its branch offices serve, and for its associate members and clients.

Created in 1911 by a decree-law that regulated the foundation and activity of agricultural savings banks, Crédito Agrícola has become deeply rooted in Portuguese society. Today it comprises a network of approximately 700 branch offices, 5,000 employees, more than 400,000 associate members and 1.2 million clients.

Agricultural savings banks form the basis of the Crédito Agrícola Group, boosting economic activity in the regions where they are located, and guaranteeing a close relationship between client and customer. Funds are generally invested in projects that deliver socio-economic benefits to the region in which the funds were raised.

INDIA

INDIAN FARMERS FERTILISER COOPERATIVE LTD (IFFCO)

With the spirit of a tireless pioneer, Indian Farmers Fertiliser Cooperative Ltd (IFFCO) has committed itself to achieving its prime role of providing quality fertilisers and agricultural services to India's farming community.

IFFCO was incorporated as a multi-state co-operative society in 1967, and registered under the *Multi State Cooperative Society Act 1984*. Over the years, this co-operative has evolved into a gigantic Indian multinational. IFFCO has set records for excellent and consistent performance in production, marketing and services to farmers, and has won several prestigious awards. It has turned into a co-operative that is truly 'Of the Farmers', 'By the Farmers' and 'For the Farmers' and has become a role model for others on the path to economic development.

IFFCO has steadily grown in strength and stature from a modest membership of 57 societies in 1967–1968 to almost 40,000 societies, and more than 6,000 employees, in the year 2011–2012. The initial equity capital of USD 11,742 contributed by the co-operatives had risen to USD 95.40 million in 2011–2012. IFFCO's plants rolled out 8.42 million metric tonnes of fertiliser material during 2011–2012. Nearly every third bag of fertiliser produced and sold in India belongs to IFFCO.

The marketing of its fertiliser products is channelled through each of its member co-operative societies, marketing federations and 158 Farmers Service Centres spread over 29 States and Union Territories across India.

Always a visionary, IFFCO has remained zealously devoted to its explicit mission of bringing incremental value within the reach of India's farming millions by creating opportunities that spell business success for the society and enhance the standard of life of farmers.

Strengthening the nation's co-operative fabric has been IFFCO's principal forte. In order to further improve the economic viability of its member co-operative societies, IFFCO has been developing some of them as 'IFFCO Franchisees' – giving them the business of

rake handling, transporting and warehousing IFFCO fertilisers, while providing guidance on educational and promotional activities. In order to recognise the efforts of co-operators, IFFCO has instituted the Sahakarita Ratan and Sahakarita Bandhu Awards. Lectures on Co-operation in memory of India's former prime minister Pandit Jawaharlal Nehru have been regularly arranged since 1982.

IFFCO has always advocated for balanced fertilisation. The society firmly believes in the urgent need to replenish the required micronutrients and secondary nutrients, which have been constantly depleted. It has therefore launched a campaign named 'Save the Soil' to emphasise soil rejuvenation and crop productivity enhancement through activities such as soil testing, reclamation of problematic soils, on-farm preparation of organic manure, vermicompost, Phospho-Sulpho-Nitro-Compost, crop diversification, and introduction of pulses in the cropping system.

The results of this campaign have been very encouraging, as crop productivity in project areas has risen by 25 percent on average.

IFFCO has thus encouraged more and more farmers to take up green manure crops for incorporation in soil to improve soil fertility.

In January 2003, IFFCO founded a think tank, the IFFCO Foundation, with the aim of strengthening co-operative structure, developing social capital and human resources and promoting cultural development through co-operative organisations, empowering women and youth, developing micro enterprise and micro credit concepts and pioneering reforms and advancements in co-operatives.

The Government of India has recognised the IFFCO Foundation as a National Level Agency for implementing a co-operative horticulture program. IFFCO has also established the IFFCO Kisan Sewa charitable trust to provide relief and rehabilitation to victims of natural calamities, and to provide welfare and critical medical attention to needy farmers.

Today, IFFCO upholds its unique blend of corporate functioning with co-operative spirit, and is breaking its own production records

to emerge as a global leader in the production and marketing of fertilisers, thereby playing a major role in the overall development of the nation with a focus on rural development. Very recently, the Indian edition of *Fortune* magazine ranked IFFCO at the head of the 'Fertilisers and Agrochemicals' category and IFFCO was the only co-operative society among the top 50 Indian companies in this ranking.

Under its VISION 2015, IFFCO desires to become a global leader in fertiliser production to cater to the food security needs of the nation. In doing so, it promotes integrated nutrient management to improve the efficiency of fertiliser use and encourages location-specific research and efficient fertiliser practices.

BRUSSELS, BELGIUM

When the P&V co-operative insurance group decided to double its size by buying the brokering arm of the Dutch-based finance institution ING's Belgium operations, it did not realise that the global financial crisis was about to hit. There can hardly be a clearer demonstration of the resilience of the co-operative insurance model.

Hilde Vernaillen, CEO of P&V, said from its headquarters in Brussels, "The group came through the crisis relatively unharmed. We have been able to get through the tough and unexpected crises of the past years thanks to our long-term focus and careful investment policy." Vernaillen, who has headed the insurance group since 2011, says, "This is a consequence of the fact that we need to be self-sufficient to finance our development".

Accessing financial markets is more difficult for co-operatives than for most banks, but P&V, originally named Prévoyance Sociale, has always been able to count on external capital when needed. Finance providers recognise the strength of the role it plays in the greater global insurance community.

"The first involvements of the Prévoyance Sociale on an international level in the early 1920s were jump-started by the need to look for reinsurance partners within the co-operative movement," explains Vernaillen. "Joseph Lemaire, President of the Prévoyance Sociale at the time and an exponent of the social democratic movement, was not happy that, until then, he had no choice but to reinsure large risks with Belgian PLC companies."

So, in 1922, Lemaire began to contact foreign co-operative insurers, which led to the establishment of an insurance committee within the International Co-operative Alliance. This later became ICMIF (the International Cooperative and Mutual Insurance Federation).

"From the start, this committee was also a platform for the exchange of information and best practices and the spreading of the co-operative and mutual message," says Vernaillen. "Today, the P&V Group still attaches importance to the international dimension of the co-operative movement."

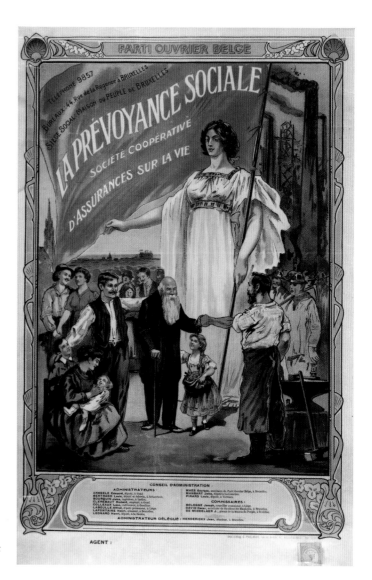

GITHUNGURI, KENYA

The Githunguri Dairy Farmers Co-operative Society has revolutionised the Kenyan dairy industry. It was formed in 1961 by 31 dairy farmers keen to improve their dairying and marketing possibilities.

Today, the co-operative has about 17,000 members, and its collection centres have expanded from one to 68.

Commissioning its own milk processing facility in 2004 led to an increase in profitability and size. Two years later, Githunguri was awarded the 'most improved company' at the national Company of the Year Awards.

Its Fresha milk is now the leading fresh milk brand in and around the Kenyan capital of Nairobi. Contributing to its dramatic growth has been its adherence to quality standards, a turnaround from previous milk production in the country.

Milk production provides a higher return for farmers per farm unit than other agricultural sectors in Kenya, such as banana, tea and coffee farming. Membership of the co-operative society also has the advantage that it provides a steady income flow.

With production at about 170,000 litres of milk a day, Githunguri is Kenya's third biggest dairy operation. The Fresha brand of products – including yoghurt, butter, ghee and cream – has changed the face of the dairy industry in Kenya.

This story was made possible with the assistance of the Swedish Cooperative Centre.

WESTERN AUSTRALIA; SOUTHEAST ASIA

CBH GROUP

Mick Gayfer, the longest-serving Chairman of what is now the CBH Group, was a passionate believer in his father's maxim, "True co-operation is a unity of many minds towards a common ideal". This captures the spirit and journey of the organisation first registered as Co-operative Bulk Handling in 1933.

Today the CBH Group, owned by around 4,500 Western Australian grain growers, is Australia's largest co-operative and a leader in the Australian grain industry, with operations extending from storage, handling and transport to marketing and processing. CBH receives and warehouses 95 percent of the grain produced in Western Australia, is the biggest exporter of grain from Western Australia and one of the top four grain exporters in the country. It is also one of Western Australia's biggest businesses, with assets of more than AUD 1.5 billion and a permanent workforce of around 900, supported by up to 1,500 casual employees during the harvest from October to January.

Its infrastructure includes more than 190 grain receival sites across southern Western Australia, four port terminals and, as of 2012, the most contemporary, efficient, dedicated grain rail fleet in the world. In the 2011 season CBH received record deliveries from growers totaling 15 million tonnes. It is a long way from its maiden season in 1932–33 when it received 42,578 tonnes of wheat.

Like many co-operatives, CBH was formed for "defensive" reasons, and its story in many ways parallels the development and expansion of agriculture in Western Australia.

CBH was born out of the hopelessness and adversity of the global Great Depression of the 1920s and early 1930s. As Cyril Ayris wrote in a history of the company published in 2000, "They were terrible times, the like of which have not been seen again in Australia, yet it was largely because of them that Co-operative Bulk Handling came into being".

The bottom line, as Ayris put it, was that farmers who were facing ruin could probably trade their way out of debt if they could reduce their crippling costs. One of their biggest costs was the traditional method of storing and moving wheat in bags that were hand-filled and carefully sewn closed with needle and twine. The answer, it was argued, might be to convert to a bulk handling system using bulk storage facilities and enclosed rail wagons.

One of the strongest supporters of bulk handling was John Thomson, the General Manager of Westralian Farmers, another co-operative that later became one of Australia's biggest and most successful listed companies, Wesfarmers. In 1932, Wesfarmers decided to go it alone and build five 14,000 tonne experimental horizontal 'bins' in the Wyalkatchem area. In April 1933, Wesfarmers and the trustees of the Wheat Pool of Western Australia jointly registered Co-operative Bulk Handling with an authorised capital of 100,000 pounds divided into 100,000 shares. By 1943, CBH had repaid all its start-up debt and control was handed over to growers.

Today CBH remains controlled by growers and focused solely on their interests. The difference is that the co-operative now has 20 million tonnes of storage and handling capacity, equity of more than AUD 1 billion and a grain marketing arm that exports to more than 20 countries. In addition, CBH owns a 50 percent stake in Interflour, one of Southeast Asia's biggest flour milling operations with four flour mills in Malaysia, a mill and grain port terminal in Vietnam and PT Eastern Flour Mills in Indonesia, the fourth-largest flour miller in the world.

Yet CBH's purpose in 2012 remains essentially the same as when it started – to create and return value to growers. The storage and handling network in Western Australia remains its core asset and the one most valued by its grower members. Many describe it as an extension of their business – they rank nothing more important than having an efficient, secure, low-cost receival and storage site within reasonable distance of their farms at harvest.

In 2002, CBH moved into grain marketing through a merger with another grower-controlled organisation, the Grain Pool of Western Australia, established in 1922. Today CBH Grain is one of Australia's leading grain marketing and trading entities, marketing more than six million tonnes annually. Aided by additional grain accumulation offices in eastern Australia and marketing offices in Hong Kong and Tokyo, CBH Grain exports wheat, barley, oats, canola, lupins and other pulses to more than 20 major markets of the world.

In 2011 CBH entered an exciting new era in grain transport by signing an agreement with USA-based Watco and investing AUD 175 million in 22 locomotives and 574 wagons. This provides Western Australian growers with the most modern and efficient grain fleet in Australia and ensures grain transported by rail remains competitive with road.

For the second year in a row, in 2011, CBH Group was named as Australia's No.1 Co-operative in the annual Top 100 list of Co-operatives, Credit Unions and Mutuals released by Co-operatives Australia.

In addition to the direct support provided to rural economies by its business activities, CBH Group is a strong supporter of rural and regional communities, industry groups and events. It provides more than AUD 250,000 annually in sponsorship and donations to improve the health and wellbeing of people living in rural regions.

The co-operative has also done all it could to help farmers and others in times of extreme challenge. This included coordinating a seed donation program during the last two major droughts in Western Australia in 2007–2008 and in 2010–2011.

In what has become a highly competitive, volatile environment, CBH is competing successfully in a marketplace now dominated by huge multinational firms many times its size. Rather than seeing its co-operative structure as a disadvantage, CBH's current CEO, Dr Andrew Crane, says it is a strength.

"From a strategic perspective, there is plenty of evidence that co-ops can be just as successful as any corporate model provided they can adapt to their changing environment. This structure helps us compete against bigger international grain businesses because it makes us different. We alone give the value we create back to the same growers who do the business with us, rather than to some distant shareholders.

"Whether CBH should remain a co-operative or corporatise has been the subject of discussion in country pubs and grower meetings for some years. Over the past two years we have done a lot of work with the board and growers to thrash this out once and for all. A detailed grower survey told us that growers wanted to retain control of their business and wanted the value to come back to them in ways other than selling shares in their business. This led to the simple but key decision that CBH would remain a co-operative. But that was only one step. We then needed to learn about the different types of co-operatives and why they succeed, and, more importantly, why they fail. Based on that work we decided to bring our constitution in line with a non-distributing co-operative model.

"We can now go and compete with companies, large and small, emphasising that we are the only ones here genuinely for growers with no other shareholders or focus. That's both powerful and unique."

TORONTO, CANADA
THE BIG CARROT

"It is so much more a participatory way of doing business," is how Heather Barclay, longtime member and current President of the Board of The Big Carrot Natural Food Market, sums up the co-operative form of commerce.

The Big Carrot is an icon in Toronto, Canada, for its organic produce (sourced from co-operative producers where possible) and for its excellent customer service, which began back in 1983. Of its 185 staff, 65 are worker-owners of the store.

The Big Carrot is also known for what it gives back to its community. A visionary commercial real estate developer, David Walsh, built a mall in the heart of Toronto that now houses the co-operative and is known as the Carrot Common Mall. Walsh initiated a deal for the co-operative to receive a third of the profits from the mall. This income is not reinvested in The Big Carrot's own business but instead is distributed to co-operative businesses generally.

"Carrot Cache Community Resources is something we are very proud of," says Barclay. "We give that money to other co-ops to start up." The Big Carrot also funds local organic food initiatives that grow the sector and sustain the web of connections necessary for long-term success. Most of the money is distributed through a system of grants. Carrot Cache is a model showing how business profits can be used for community building and to further long-term agricultural and food security goals.

There are not many worker co-operatives in Canada, explains Barclay. The Big Carrot has an assembly of its members once every two weeks. "It sometimes gets a bit contentious in meetings, but people respect the democratic process," says Barclay. "At least you feel you have some say.

"I think people are looking and realising that the traditional corporate style isn't working in the long run," she says. "People are looking for more than a wage out of their work."

About six years ago the Big Carrot undertook a major expansion and renovation of its store. "We revamped the inside of the store and our sales shot up after this," says Barclay. The co-operative has considered how to follow up that success, and is now becoming involved in outside projects.

"We are very involved in the non-GMO [Genetically Modified Organisms] project," says Barclay. One of its members is on that project's board. The Big Carrot recently became a certified organic retailer. "We're proud of that because it speaks to our credibility and what our customers expect of us." It also offers cooking classes, nutritional store tours and free weekly lectures on health and the environment.

The income from the mall has helped the co-operative to build a 'green roof' on the Carrot Common mall – an urban gardening and community resource centre including several types of roof-top gardens, a university research garden, demonstration kitchen and other urban agriculture resources.

Whichever way it moves, The Big Carrot is always improving.

This page: CARD (Centre for Agricultural and Rural Development), Philippines.

CHAPTER 8

Inspiring change

MONDRAGÓN, SPAIN

In post-civil war Spain's Basque country, a group of working class students with few job prospects founded a small co-operative to build paraffin stoves. They then began to set up other co-operative business ventures. When they needed capital for expansion, they started their own co-operative bank.

These students had been taught the ways of the Catholic priest José María Arizmendiarrieta, whose beliefs were rooted in solidarity. In 1943 he began a training college in the small Basque town of Mondragón, which became the seed for the many co-operatives that have come to dominate the Basque economy.

By the end of 1990, the now-merged co-operatives of Mondragón and its surrounds employed around 23,000 workers. Over the following two decades this number grew to more than 85,000, some 85 percent of whom were members of the main Mondragón co-operative.

Today the same difficulties that inspired the co-operatives of Mondragón in the 1940s are affecting the lives of workers in the USA – lack of jobs, creeping poverty and distrust of the economic and political system. Unsurprisingly, therefore, the United Steelworkers Union has set up a partnership with Mondragón, aimed at setting up workers' co-operatives in the USA.

GERMANY

Germans were able to celebrate the arrival of the 21st century with green electricity.

The story of Germany's largest independent energy co-operative began with the liberalisation of energy markets back in the 1990s.

Greenpeace Energy grew out of the environmental protection organisation Greenpeace's desire to see high quality, green electricity. Its campaign attracted swathes of supporters looking for clean energy, and the organisation then began a public tender process. When no single supplier could meet all of its criteria, the worldwide organisation set up – at arm's length – a co-operative, Greenpeace Energy.

A year after it made green electricity available in 2000, Greenpeace Energy launched Planet Energy to build clean power plants.

"Here in Germany everybody is talking about the Energiewende [energy turnaround] now, but we are the ones who know how to realise this energy turnaround," says Henrik Düker of Greenpeace Energy. "For example, in 2001 we launched our new product proWindgas, a renewable gas made out of wind energy.

"Its key technology is the conversion of green electricity – especially wind power – into hydrogen. Greenpeace Energy is thus pressing ahead with an innovative storage technology for renewable energy."

How was this clean energy supplier able to set its ecologically committed business policy in stone?

The answer is simple – it is a co-operative.

WESTERN CANADA
FEDERATED CO-OPERATIVES LIMITED (FCL)

In 2010, Scott Banda sat before the board of Federated Co-operatives Limited (FCL) and delivered a message to each director. If he was to be their choice of CEO, the board had to have an appetite for initiatives to make FCL more competitive because "the only constant we have is change". He told the board, "If you want status quo, I'm not your guy".

FCL had been operating for more than 80 years, and the past 15 had seen particularly good financial success. "We've had a great history, we've got a great reputation out there," says the President of the Board, Glen Tully. But FCL was facing challenges, in particular the emergence of aggressive new competition in a variety of business lines. As its competitors were consolidating around it, FCL had to question whether it needed as many service points, said Tully.

"We serve communities, but the definition of community is changing," he says. "Community was [once] how far your horse could take you in a day. Now community has become at least a 160km radius, if not further."

A number of organisational challenges also made responding to the new competition very difficult. As Banda told the board on that fateful day in January 2010, it was obvious to him that the organisation needed to change and to evolve. He explains his philosophy as, "Every day we stand still, we are falling behind".

Banda was aware of the need to compete with private sector companies and stockmarket-listed bodies, which move at a fast pace and are constantly dreaming up different ways to market themselves and their products. "The biggest challenge we have is to lead the evolution of an organisation," he says. "We need to evolve and we need to evolve quickly."

FCL is a CAD 8.5 billion co-operative that counts 231 members in retail operations dealing in business lines ranging from crop supplies to animal feeds, food to hardware, and bulk petroleum to pharmacy. These retailers range in size from CAD 1 billion in annual sales (the Calgary Co-op, profiled elsewhere in this publication) to less than CAD 1 million in sales. Each of these independent co-operatives collectively form the ownership of FCL and have a presence in more than 500 communities in western Canada. Together with FCL itself, they comprise the Co-operative Retailing System (CRS).

FCL provides its retail member owners with support in areas such as marketing, information technology, distribution and logistics, and human resources. FCL also manufactures gasoline and diesel products through the operation of Canada's fourth largest petroleum refinery, the Co-op Refinery Complex, a wholly owned subsidiary located in Regina, Saskatchewan. "We exist because of our passion, but a lot of our profitability is in petroleum," said Tully.

Banda's first step after being appointed to lead FCL was to make changes in how the management team functioned. "I took it from a senior management team to a senior leadership team." The senior leadership of the company needed to consider more strategic aspects of the challenges ahead, and to empower employees in a way previously not practised. Tully says that when the management team stepped up to newfound freedoms and responsibilities, the board recognised that it needed to do the same.

Tully, who has been involved with FCL since 1995, stressed that Banda needed a board that would back him, but that the board also needed to evolve – to become more strategic as opposed to focusing on operational considerations.

On top of its hard-driven evolution to be more competitive in specific business lines, FCL is also pursuing three major change initiatives. "We've layered on three massive transformational projects," says Banda.

The first is talent management. Finding and keeping good people have been vital parts of the strategy that Banda is working towards. This involves creating a comprehensive Performance Management System that encompasses all aspects of human resource management, including the development and application of a competency based system that will improve all aspects

of recruitment, training and development. Linked to this is the implementation of a Total Rewards System that will help ensure that FCL remains competitive across a range of sectors, not only retail and wholesale.

The second 'transformational project' for FCL concerns its brand and how it communicates co-operative values. "We've had great raw data but we haven't had a communications strategy, all of which is now changing. It's how the public sees us and how we see ourselves internally," Banda explains. "(But) our research tells us that we haven't told our story very well or often enough."

The new CEO makes an important distinction. "We don't have to re-invent ourselves, we just have to re-introduce ourselves."

FCL has enormously strong relationships with its members, and local co-operatives in the Co-operative Retailing System have very strong and trusted positions in the communities where they operate. It is these co-operatives' investment in, and commitment to, their communities that form one of the foundations of the reinvigorated

brand. FCL's research shows clearly that co-operatives are trusted, respected, and "are the kind of business [people] want in their community". This is a critical brand advantage that Banda believes the CRS can leverage into a competitive advantage.

"We have an intimate relationship with the majority of our members," says Banda. "This is where the democratic aspect of our co-operative is an advantage. It's not enough to talk about our brand; we have to live it. We are trying; there is not a day when there is not a major challenge that we face."

This democratic model may mean that annual meetings invite a great many more questions from delegates than is typical for a stockmarket-listed company, but as a result the board and leadership team have more accountability and are more focused on the CRS's values.

Above: Service with a smile ... then and now.

Our Vision declares: Federated Co-operatives Limited will set the world standard in consumer co-operative excellence.

Our Mission states: To provide responsible, innovative leadership and support to the Co-operative Retailing System, for the benefit of members, employees and Canadian communities.

Its final transformational project is technology. FCL's single biggest challenge, and one of its biggest expenses, explains Tully, is to make the necessary changes to the organisation's information technology infrastructure.

Banda elaborates: "This is not an area we've done well in, we're in catch-up mode. Not only that but we have to do some leapfrogging."

Projects in this area include enhanced business analytics, better human resource information systems, unified point of sale systems, and the list goes on. The bottom line is that FCL and the CRS recognise that significant investments need to be made in order to keep pace with, and even outstrip, the competition.

"The good news," says Banda, "is that because we didn't focus on some of these information technology challenges for so long, we don't have many legacy systems to slow down our implementation of solutions.

We are in a position to learn from others and implement 'best of breed' solutions now, that will position us very well for the future."

The three transformational plans are well embedded in an overarching timetable. Banda says 2011 was devoted to research, and 2012 is devoted to developing the concepts behind its transformation. Next year, 2013, is all about a rollout phase of many of the new processes and concepts.

As for its global positioning, Banda asserts that the 2008 financial crisis has shown that "how you act matters".

"We have to understand our appeal isn't within an organisation, our values are (our appeal). Integrity, excellence, responsibility – we ask that they be the filter of every decision that you make." He adds that these very values dovetail nicely into co-operative values globally. "This is all about the next generation," Banda concludes. He and his team are building something for the next generation of Western Canada's co-operators. Scott Banda has a simple vision. "I want to come in here one morning and see everyone smiling [because] they have an opportunity to be appreciated, to be listened to and see that together we will build something pretty special."

FCL's vision for its next 10 years declares that it will set the world standard in consumer co-operative excellence, and will aspire to 'exemplary organisational governance, modelling of democratic principles and co-operative values'. It aims to create 'broad consumer awareness and positive perceptions of the Co-op brand and its products and services', to have 'best-in-class member loyalty', and to model 'outstanding employee engagement levels'. It sees itself gaining a 'growing market presence and relevance in urban Canada' and being a 'market leader in rural Canada'. It hopes to achieve 'consistently strong financial performance' and to set the standard on 'environmentally responsible practices and products'. Co-op's mission is to be a 'vital economic and social force in our home communities', and it states that it will endeavour to 'provide responsible, innovative leadership and to support to the co-operative retailing system, for the benefit of its members, employees and Canadian communities'.

Opposite page: FCL/CRS initiatives support many community causes including the Canadian Breast Cancer Foundation.

Top left: FCL CEO Scott Banda (Back row 3rd from left) celebrates with colleagues participating in "Path to Performance" talent management initiative.

Top right: FCL President Glen Tully addresses elected delegates to the 2012 annual meeting.

You're at home here.

JAPAN

Sanchoku translates as 'direct transaction from producer to consumer'. It is a business model championed by Japanese consumer co-operatives that aims to ensure high standards in farming and food production.

Sanchoku is agriculture supported by the community. It ensures stable procurement of food supplies. It is also one of the co-operative methods advocated for areas affected by the Great East Japan earthquake of 2011. A revival of sanchoku in this region could help quicken the pace of recovery, according to Tokyo University Graduate College Associate Professor Hiroyasu Nakashima.

For the consumer co-operatives – with more than 26 million members representing more than 35 percent of Japanese households – working towards sanchoku involves working to improve the safety and security of life.

The Taro Fisheries Co-op is an association of fishermen that works to maintain environmentally sustainable production of toxin-free seaweed and other aquatic plants, including wakame seaweed.

The working facilities of the co-operative suffered catastrophic damage in the earthquake. All of the fishing villages and ports from which it operated were damaged. Taro is working on the reconstruction and revival of the business with strong support from its individual and federation members, and local government.

The co-operative supports the regional fishery through projects such as tree-planting, which will reduce water pollution in coastal areas.

Its members' focus is on supplying safe, healthy and nutritious seaweed for direct sale to consumers – a perfect example of sanchoku in action.

NADI, FIJI

Sant Kumar is now retired from the Natures Way Co-operative – as retired as a persistent, energetic fellow can be.

Among his other activities, Kumar still grows seedlings for the service co-operative he helped to found. The Natures Way Co-operative provides quarantine treatment for its fruit and vegetable farmer members, particularly those that export their product. It therefore needs a consistent supply of papaya, mango, eggplant and breadfruit.

Since the co-operative was founded in 1995, it has grown from treating 30 tonnes of papaya to 1,300 tonnes of mixed production annually. In his retirement, Kumar does his best to ensure that supply can meet the burgeoning demand.

Fiji, where the Natures Way Co-operative is based, is facing significant economic change. The 100-year-old sugar cane plantation system is disappearing, and many Fijian Indian farmers are seeing their land returned to native Fijians as their leases expire.

Papaya growing, once the domain of private gardeners, has moved into mainstream production. According to Kumar, demand from overseas markets has caused this industry to take off.

Transporting their products from Fijian soil to their overseas destination has been the greatest challenge for smaller landholders. Expensive quarantine treatment, complex food safety requirements, limited access to transport and competition from larger countries have all been prohibitive. Natures Way stepped in, assumed responsibility for those activities and made this sector of Fijian agriculture far more profitable. Fiji now exports more than 200 different agricultural products to more than 20 countries.

This almost didn't happen. When Natures Way was established in 1995 in order to open the quarantine treatment facility, co-operatives were not commonly accepted in the Pacific. The United States Agency for International Development (USAID) had provided the funds for the new treatment plant on condition that it would be privately owned, so the decision to choose a co-operative structure created significant difficulties.

Commercial banks, and the International Finance Corporation, refused to finance the co-operative. Without Kumar's resolve the start-up capital would never have been found. A visit from New Zealand's then-minister of foreign affairs, Don McKinnon, proved to be the stroke of luck the initiative needed.

McKinnon recognised the value of the project, Kumar recalls with a chuckle, and ensured that the money came through.

LAGUNA, PHILIPPINES

I guess we are very lucky in the Philippines because our insurance commission has been very supportive of the kind of work that we do. They believe that empowering the poor by giving them ownership of micro-insurance companies is the best [means of] poverty eradication.

— ARIS ALIP

Aris Alip is the founder of Centre for Agricultural and Rural Development – Mutually Reinforcing Institutions (CARD MRI). One of its nine mutually reinforcing members, CARD MBA (Mutual Benefit Association), has been behind the development of the micro-insurance industry, not only in the Philippines but throughout Southeast Asia.

In April 1988, CARD began its operations with a training and livelihood assistance program for landless coconut workers. Eight months later, CARD pilot-tested a scheme modified from India's pioneering Grameen Bank in four villages of San Pablo City, Laguna. After much success it moved into an official program in 1990.

In support of CARD's goal to empower members, the management of the Members' Mutual Fund was officially turned over to the members in 1999 during a two-day workshop held in San Pablo City. From then on the fund was called the CARD Mutual Benefit Association, Inc. (CARD MBA), a separate legal entity owned and managed by the members.

The co-operative model of insurance has been so successful that CARD MBA has introduced it in other Asian countries, including Vietnam, Cambodia and Indonesia.

"We're also pursuing opportunities in Laos, and we will go to Myanmar so we can replicate the CARD MBA model there," says Alip. He is keenly aware of the need to work with governments outside of the Philippines to create the kind of policy environment in which co-operatives can flourish.

While supporting the goal of growth, Alip is also a strong proponent of the need to introduce high standards in the micro-insurance industry.

"It is a specialised industry, which needs a responsive touch," he says. "CARD MBA tries to pay all claims within a day, or three to five days at the maximum, because when you're dealing with the poor, getting the funds to them when they need them most is very important."

BOLOGNA, ITALY

In November 2011 Italy was on the brink of economic collapse, with bond markets set to send the country tumbling into insolvency. Government and regulators were asked to act incisively and responsibly to re-establish the confidence of financial markets in the country. A volatile market made it difficult to make even short-term financial forecasts.

One month later Italy's fourth largest insurance group, Unipol, took a stand.

In the face of the nation's crippling financial situation and its people's uncertainty about the future, this stockmarket-listed company, which is majority controlled by about 40 Italian co-operatives, sent a message of hope to the people of Italy.

It launched an online campaign inviting people to post comments and exchange opinions to help provide Italy with a burst of positive energy. It also advertised in subways, in newspapers, in magazines.

Unipol then published the most interesting messages, which promoted participation and increased awareness of its campaign.

In response, it received the following call from 36-year-old Stefano Nicoletti from Tuscany.

"I have confidence in the future because I accept responsibility and take it on my shoulders all the time, even when I get tired and bruised."

Unipol responded, "We strongly believe that such messages of faith in the future provide the most extraordinary and inexhaustible basis for tackling the current situation and getting the country back on its feet."

NOVA PETRÓPOLIS, BRAZIL

If a huge stone is in the way of 20 people, they could not pass if they individually tried to remove it. However, if the 20 people came together and worked under the orientation of one of them, jointly they could remove the stone and open the way to everyone.

– THEODOR AMISTAD

Theodor Amistad, a priest, was a firm believer in the principle of co-operation between human beings. It was the reason he founded the first credit co-operative in Latin America in 1902. As with his story about the huge stone, Father Amistad's decision to begin a co-operative not only brought people together around a common objective. In addition, solidarity and tolerance became their means of achieving it.

Sicredi Pioneira RS, with a membership of 70,000, is one of the 116 credit co-operatives in the historic and powerful Sicredi organisation, founded by Amistad in Nova Petrópolis in southern Brazil. This German settlement is regarded as the capital of the co-operative movement in Brazil.

While Sicredi Pioneira RS has a famous history, it also has an eye on the future. It is a supporter of Scholar Co-operatives, a program that encourages students to organise themselves into co-operatives.

This initiative not only breeds future managers and community leaders in Brazil, it educates community members about Amistad's original principle of co-operation.

Aptly, a stone monument telling Amistad's story was erected on the 100th anniversary of the founding of what is the continent's first credit union.

ASUNCIÓN, PARAGUAY

Paraguay is sometimes referred to as Corazón de América, or the Heart of America. In recent times it has boasted the world's second fastest growing economy.

A large proportion of Paraguay's population derives its income from agriculture, much of it from subsistence farming. The country is the sixth largest soya bean supplier in the world.

In 2008 a drought wreaked havoc on the farmers. Tajy, a co-operative Paraguayan insurer, responded to the farmers' demand for insurance in co-operation with the Federation of Producer Co-operatives and another co-operative insurer, Grupo Aseguradora La Segunda of Argentina, which contributed the expertise it had gained providing insurance to Argentinean farmers for 78 years.

As well as promoting safe production areas and supervising work practices, the collective insurance scheme has allowed Tajy to move into new business areas and reinsurance. It was able to expand its range of cover for soya bean production after successfully insuring the first two crops.

The success of the model is demonstrated by the number of soya producers insured in Paraguay, which jumped 359 percent from 2010 to 2011.

ARNHEM LAND, AUSTRALIA

In the wet season you need a light plane to travel from Darwin to many parts of Arnhem Land. Even in the dry season you have to watch for the tides and crocodiles.

For the staff of the Traditional Credit Union (TCU), the only business offering banking services to 11 Indigenous communities in this remote region of northern Australia, leaving their Darwin head office to visit the branches can be a week-long expedition.

But the services the credit union provides are vital. They enable members to save their money (and the very concept of money is difficult to grasp for many members of these traditional communities). The credit union has also significantly increased training and job possibilities for members of the local community.

As Sam Wees, a TCU branch supervisor, explains: "My brother had told me that the elders told him about a banking job at the credit union. At first I didn't want it because I was happy working for Power & Water and thought office work was a woman's job, and men worked outdoors. But that changed when he told me that if I didn't take it they would close the branch and the community would have no bank, so I took the job to keep the bank in the community."

This Aboriginal community did manage to keep its bank, and thanks in part to the opportunity provided by the TCU, Wees went on to win the 2011 Northern Territory Training Award for Aboriginal and Torres Strait Islander Student of the Year.

"I feel that this is a great achievement for me, as my family and community life can provide a lot of distractions and reasons not to see my study through to the end," says Wees. "My confidence has grown over the period of my traineeship, and I've shown genuine commitment to share the knowledge that I have gained with my family and friends in the community. So, no matter what your age, your level of schooling or where you are living, anything can be done if you really want it."

Top left: Photography James Fisher/Copyright Tourism Australia.
Top right: Mt Borradaile, Arnhem Land, NT, Copyright Tourism Australia.
Opposite page: Photography James Fisher/Copyright Tourism Australia.

This page: A young girl waits in a train carriage at the Kamalapur Railway Station, Bangladesh. Right: Traditional Mayan fabric, El Salvador.

CHAPTER 9

Delivering benefits

JAPAN

The word for rice in Japanese is *gohan*. It's also the word used in Japan for a meal.

Rice is so valuable in Japanese society that it was once even used as a form of currency.

In a bid for greater self-sufficiency, in 2009 the members of the Hikari Jigyodan co-operative in the far south of Japan began to grow their own rice. Little did they realise the value those grains would later come to hold.

On 11 March 2011, at 2.45pm, one of the most powerful earthquakes ever to afflict Japan rocked the northeastern part of its most populous island, Honshu. Buildings shook in Tokyo, 200km to the south of the epicentre. A seven metre high tsunami followed, destroying villages, damaging the fishing industry and washing agricultural lands out to sea.

Eight months later, members of Hikari Jigyodan – part of the Japanese Worker's Co-operative Union (JWCU) – made the day-long drive to the north of Honshu. They were bringing 60 kilos of their rice

to fellow JWCU members in the Ishinomaki Jigyodan co-operative. This co-operative's office, and in some cases its members' livelihoods, had been washed away by the tsunami. The sticky rice cakes the two organisations prepared, then ate together, were a potent symbol of their co-operation.

SAN JOSÉ, COSTA RICA

It was a rural schoolteacher, Alejandro Rodríguez, who first raised the idea of a collectively owned institution in Costa Rica.

The year was 1920 and the country was newly freed from the unhappy reign of military dictator General Federico Tinoco Granados. After Granados was overthrown, the unpopularity of his regime led to a steep decline in the prosperity and influence of the Costa Rican military.

This provided Rodríguez and his supporters with an opportunity to form Sociedad de Seguros de Vida del Magisterio Nacional (SSVMN). Legislation was passed and before long 2,000 Costa Rican teachers were insured.

Costa Rica is Spanish for 'rich coast', yet in 1719 a Spanish Governor described it as "the poorest and most miserable Spanish colony in all America". For the conquistadores it was indeed a poor place, and lacked sufficient indigenous people to work on the colonists' haciendas. This meant that Costa Rica developed its own rural democracy, which has ensured its high position in the Human Development Index relative to other Latin American countries.

Ninety years on, SSVMN now provides insurance for nearly 25 percent of the Costa Rican population. Life insurance is compulsory for Costa Rican education professionals and education is Costa Rica's largest employer, with 75,000 people working in this sector. This translates to one or two active or pensioned education professionals in nearly every family in Costa Rica. SSVMN has 145,000 insured members who in turn have 845,000 beneficiaries, totalling 990,000.

"We provide financial protection through technical provisions and catastrophic insurance that ensures the payment of mutual insurance, as well as making available services such as loans, grants, orthopedic equipment and advances policy to the policyholders," SSVMN explains.

In January 2012 the insurer was certified under the ISO series 9000, designed to measure quality of management in meeting customers' and members' needs.

"The work just begins – there is still a long way to go. But with a clear objective and clear standards, the improvement continues."

BANGLADESH

It may be a national holiday, and offices across the country are closed, but you might still find Jim Ford at his desk.

The development expert worked in the field for the USA National Rural Electric Cooperative Association (NRECA) for decades. He spent many years in Bangladesh directing technical assistance projects for a rural electrification program, funded by the USA Government through the United States Agency for International Development (USAID), and delivered by NRECA.

"It's clear that having access to electricity is a catalyst for economic development," says Ford. "Many rural people thought at the beginning that they would never get electricity and consequently it was initially difficult getting people to sign up to be member-consumers."

But need electricity they did. In Bangladesh, 90 percent of the population lives in rural districts and there are about 80,000 rural villages. One of many positive side-effects of the electrification program is the greater number of jobs in these areas, which has significantly reduced migration to the cities.

"Considering the size of the program, it's been remarkably successful," says Ford. In fact, many people have identified it as the most successful rural-electrification program in Southeast Asia to date. In addition to USAID, 14 other development partners have provided financial support for this program.

"It's been one place that you've really seen it emerge from very small into something very significant," says Ford. The program followed the NRECA co-operative model that electrified rural America, and there are now 70 rural electric distribution systems operating on co-operative principles in Bangladesh. "At the beginning rural people didn't dream it was possible to have electricity in their villages.

"It is a credit to the people of Bangladesh who contributed to this effort, many of whom dedicated their entire careers to making the dream possible for millions of their fellow citizens. I had the good fortune of being involved in such a program that touches people's lives – and it continues to touch people's lives – and it's a great feeling," concludes Ford.

PUNE, INDIA

Jayshree Bhika Naik lives in Pune, a relatively prosperous Indian city, which was once the centre of Indian politics.

Naik is one of the 30 percent of Pune residents who live in the city's slums. She works as a housemaid while her husband runs a small catering business.

Nevertheless, a slum-dwelling existence is no barrier to medical care in India. Jayshree Bhika Naik and her family are insured against illness through micro-insurance products offered by the co-operative insurer Uplift Mutuals.

This company recognises that its members not only need health cover but advice and assistance in times of need. When Naik's 12-year-old son Rahul became ill with a condition associated with high blood pressure, Uplift Mutuals took them both to hospital. Later, their insurance paid for her son's 15-day stay in a private hospital, a treatment that saved his life.

Total cost of care: INR100,000 (USD 2,222). If the Naik family had not been insured, incurring this cost would have been a dreadful outcome. In fact, Rahul's medicine was paid with a loan from the family who employed Naik as a maid, and mostly repaid when she was reimbursed by Uplift.

"I am really satisfied, very happy. Your help came like God", Naik told her insurer afterwards. "If I was not an Uplift Mutuals member, nobody would have helped me. But you gave me proper guidance. I really thank you. My boy is now safe."

STOCKHOLM, SWEDEN
HSB HOUSING CO-OPERATIVES

For a man's house is his castle; one's home is the safest refuge for all.

– ENGLISH JURIST SIR EDWARD COKE, 1644

So it was for the first members of the HSB Housing co-operatives in Sweden in the early 1900s. They felt as though their homes were finally safe refuges.

Industrialisation did not really take hold in Sweden until the 1900s, when a great need arose for urban housing for workers. The Hyresgästernas Sparkasse – och Byggnadsförening or HSB (Tenant's Savings and Construction Association), formed to meet this need.

The first HSB Housing co-op was founded in 1923 by the Tenants' Union, with the intention that the co-operative members would build and own their housing estates. Under the HSB model, the property was owned by the co-operative, which led to collective safety and security.

In the 1930s, HSB developed an extensive range of industrial activities including joinery, factories to build detached houses and developing a marble quarry.

By the 1940s and 1950s, HSB had constructed a high proportion of Sweden's municipal rental housing, as well as building its own housing co-operatives. Work expanded again in the following two

decades, when it built more than 10,000 apartments per year. Today, the HSB National Association comprises 31 regional associations representing 330,000 apartments and 550,000 members.

It has broken ground in the development of housing in Sweden. "We were building bathrooms in every apartment and common laundries as early as the 1920s," says Anders Lago, Chairman of HSB National Association.

"In order to rationalise and reduce construction costs, we introduced a special 'HSB Standard', which became a model for the standardisation of housing construction in Sweden."

In total, HBS has built about 10 percent of all housing in Sweden. It also owns the tallest building in Scandinavia, a spiralling residential skyscraper in Malmö, Sweden, known as the 'Twisting Torso'.

HSB – där möjligheterna bor

KARACHI, PAKISTAN

The story of the Karachi Co-operative Housing Societies Union Limited begins with one man.

M. Sharif Baiji grew up in the lap of co-operation. His father devoted his life to helping poor and powerless people in the Sindh region of Pakistan, home to the nation's capital, Karachi.

Since becoming a director of the Karachi Co-operative Housing Societies Union, Baiji has been behind the development of houses, flats and townships in rural and urban areas of Sindh. FairPrice shops (profiled elsewhere in this book) and other co-operative housing have since been opened.

The formation of the union has also led the way in the promotion of women's rights in co-operatives, and it has taken an active role in the International Co-operative Alliance's housing activities and committees. Karachi also gave a lot of help to refugees from the devastating floods of 2010.

As the union's mission statement says: All for each and each for all.

MONTEVIDEO, URUGUAY

Professionalism, attention, cordiality, responsibility, advice, commitment, autonomy, transparency, innovation – this is the weighty motto of the Compañia Co-operativa de Seguros (SURCO), a co-operative insurance company in Uruguay. Its president, Sergio Fuentes, describes it as building a co-operative insurance business, designed to serve generations of members for years to come.

"Above all, when we are building a company, our aim is that SURCO lasts for many, many years and generations," Fuentes says. "And, of course, we want to specially build this company on the principles and values of co-operativism."

SURCO is a Uruguayan co-operative insurance company born in 1992, out of a consolidation of several other co-operatives.

Uruguay is an attractive place to do business. It is one of the most economically advanced countries in Latin America. Transparency International rates it the second-least corrupt country in Latin America.

This commercial environment has provided ample opportunity for SURCO to expand – In 2011 its business grew by nearly 12 percent.

SURCO has a leading market position in agricultural insurance products. It insures about 30 percent of the land on which cereals and oilseeds are farmed.

"Our mission and vision are a constant guide for the making of decisions and the best management of the company," says Fuentes. "Our best practices rest on them."

BEIT SHE'AN VALLEY, ISRAEL

Olives, grapes, wheat, barley, figs, dates and pomegranates are the seven biblical crops which, it is written, would thrive in Israel's sun-baked soil.

At the Kibbutz Sde Eliyahu – the only religious kibbutz in Israel to solely rely on agriculture and related businesses – six of these seven plant varieties are cultivated. And very few pesticides are used.

The central kibbutz buildings lie amidst green lawns and mature trees. Spread out in the Beit She'an valley, which runs into the Sea of Galilee, the kibbutz is located on a migratory bird route.

Sde Eliyahu is supported by a variety of businesses. One of these is Bio-Tour, a bustling business arm of the co-operative that runs tours throughout its various agricultural operations and biological control systems.

Kibbutz Sde Eliyahu has recently taken its organic production methods a step further. It first developed a business that sells pest-devouring insects, then a business rearing bumblebees for pollinating hothouse and open field crops.

The kibbutz grew from the Youth Aliyah movement – the group that rescued Jewish children from Nazis during the Third Reich. They arrived in Israel in 1935 and established the kibbutz in 1939. Sde Eliyahu was named in honour of Rabbi Eliyahu Gutmacher, who died in 1875.

AZEZO, ETHIOPIA

The bloodstained years of the Mengistu regime from 1974 to 1991, combined with Ethiopia's drought-stricken 1980s, have been a painful ordeal for the people of this multicultural East African nation.

This is a land of vast natural beauty, yet food security and poverty are daily challenges for its population. This paradox is typified by the provincial capital city of Gondar, which lies in the green, temperate belt of the northeast, framed by the Simien mountain range. Gondar nestles more than 2,000 metres above sea level and was Ethiopia's capital until 1855. Its royal castles have given it the nickname of Africa's Camelot.

Several kilometres to its south lies the small town of Azezo. A nearby military base alongside the Demaza River has exacerbated unrest in the area. Yet Azezo's 35,000-strong population has well established co-operative solutions to cope with both natural and political challenges.

Informal co-operative structures are a part of everyday survival. Farmers form collectives known as Wobbera, Debo or Wonfel in order to manage the weeding and harvesting periods during the farming year. The farmers move collectively from one farm to another to complete these tasks.

When capital is needed an Ekub is formed. Community members gather and contribute an agreed amount of money to a pool, which is then rotated among the members throughout the year on a monthly basis.

Religious and ceremonial occasions are organised through another kind of informal co-operative known as a Mehaber. When a member marries, the co-operative contributes food, labour and money. When there is a death in the community, the funeral is organised co-operatively. Co-operative members gather together on the last Sunday of every month to socialise.

A more advanced informal co-operative is known locally as the Idir. The Association for Mutual and Emergency Help provides humanitarian support to its membership, comprised of very poor people. Founded in 1994, the Idir has its own by-laws, a nine-person elected board and regular meetings.

These co-operatives may be informal, but they are an integral part of life in this corner of the Horn of Africa.

SAN SALVADOR, EL SALVADOR

Many Salvadorians fear that taking out life insurance is tempting fate. There is also an assumption that it is only for wealthy people.

A number of Salvadorians move north to live in the USA, but wish to be returned home after death. Returning a body to El Salvador can cost as much as USD 12,000, an unaffordable burden that family are often left to carry.

El Salvador's only co-operative insurance company, Seguros Futuro, is educating Salvadorians about insurance. Its program, Propiciando los Microseguros para Receptores de Remesas, is backed by the International Labour Organization, and has been attended by more than 500 people.

Of those attending, 20 to 30 percent have taken up repatriation and remittance insurance or other life micro-insurance products, or have joined the co-operative.

"We are always looking for ways to help protect the poorest citizens, through education and insurance culture," says Seguros

Futura General Manager Daysi Rosales, who has spent 22 years working in the insurance industry in El Salvador.

An imprint of Toro Media
ABN 21 155 963 330
Level 12, 99 Walker Street
NORTH SYDNEY NSW 2060
Telephone: 61 2 8923 8000
www.focus.com.au

Focus is Australia's leading corporate and custom book publisher, producing
high-quality business and brand books, corporate histories, and specific
marketing, event, promotional and anniversary books. Focus also provides a
range of archiving, oral history and knowledge management services. For more
information about Focus Publishing, visit: www.focus.com.au

Publisher	Richard Hanney
Project Manager	Phil Jones
Editor	Mark Derby
Creative Director	Monica Lawrie

Author: Kate Askew
Title: *Building a Better World: 100 Stories of Co-operation*
ISBN: 978-1-921156-97-7

Printed in China by Imago.

ABOUT THE AUTHOR

Kate Askew has been imparting stories for much of her life.
For a couple of decades she told stories as a journalist in Australia,
from Kalgoorlie via Adelaide, Melbourne and finally Sydney. It was
there that she spent 11 years as a senior writer at *The Sydney
Morning Herald*, writing the CBD column for four years and doing her
level best to keep 'mum and dad' shareholders as informed
as the rest of the players in the stock market. It was during this
time that Kate had her first professional encounter with the
co-operative business model, a motorists' association whose
hoary story she followed for many years as it forced its way through
to demutualisation. In covering members' dissent she potentially
faced a jail sentence after being ordered by a court to answer
questions about her sources of information. The case was later
dropped by the association. Kate exposed the profligate ways of
internet entrepreneurs in her 2011 book, *Dot Bomb Australia: How
we wrangled, conned and argie-bargied our way into the new digital
universe*. And in the same year she co-designed, as an associate of
Sommerson Communications, the Euricse-ICA storytelling campaign,
www.stories.coop. Kate continues to write stories about co-operatives
through her work with the International Co-operative Alliance. She
lives with her husband Hans and three children, Otto, Kitty and
Karl, between the Black Forest and the Swabian Alps in Germany's
Neckartal. She shops and banks with local, German co-operatives.